Working with Children and Teenagers Using Solution Focused Approaches

of related interest

Communication Skills for Working with Children
Introducing Social Pedagogy
3rd Edition
Pat Petrie
ISBN 978 1 84905 137 8

Solution Focused Therapy for the Helping Professions
Barry Winbolt
ISBN 978 1 84310 970 9

Learning Through Child Observation
2nd Edition
Mary Fawcett
ISBN 978 1 84310 676 0

Social Pedagogy and Working with Children
Engaging with Children in Care
Edited by Claire Cameron and Peter Moss
ISBN 978 1 84905 119 4

Listening to Children
A Practitioner's Guide
Alison McLeod
ISBN 978 1 84310 549 7

Supporting Traumatized Children and Teenagers
A Guide to Providing Understanding and Help
Atle Dyregrov
ISBN 978 1 84905 034 0

A Practical Guide to Caring for Children and Teenagers with Attachment Difficulties
Chris Taylor
ISBN 978 1 84905 081 4

Promoting Psychological Well-Being in Children with Acute and Chronic Illness
Melinda Edwards and Penny Titman
ISBN 978 1 84310 967 9

Working with Children and Teenagers Using Solution Focused Approaches

Enabling Children to Overcome Challenges and Achieve their Potential

Judith Milner and Jackie Bateman

Jessica Kingsley *Publishers*
London and Philadelphia

First published in 2011
by Jessica Kingsley Publishers
116 Pentonville Road
London N1 9JB, UK
and
400 Market Street, Suite 400
Philadelphia, PA 19106, USA

www.jkp.com

Library of Congress Cataloging in Publication Data
A CIP catalog record for this book is available from the Library of Congress

British Library Cataloguing in Publication Data
A CIP catalogue record for this book is available from the British Library

ISBN 978 1 84905 082 1

Printed and bound in Great Britain

To Ella and Evie, George and Lulu.

Acknowledgements

There are many people to whom we owe thanks for opportunities, ideas, critical comments, practical help and enthusiastic support:

- Paul Edwards and Pat Bastian for patiently reading drafts.
- Alasdair Macdonald, Steve Myers and Lyndsey Taylor for practical help, reading, encouragement, and unfailing wit and good humour.
- Staff at Barnardo's The Junction Project.
- Stephen Jones and Caroline Walton at Jessica Kingsley Publishers for their encouragement and support.

And most importantly of all, the children and young people who allowed us to use their stories. We have disguised these stories to protect their confidentiality but hope that we still do justice to their strengths and resources in solution finding.

Contents

Chapter One

Useful Conversations

Positive approaches to working with children

In writing this book, we have endeavoured to highlight how solution focused approaches can be useful to a broad range of practitioners working with children – whether in education, health, social, family and community support, youth justice and crime prevention, sport and culture, early years or child care settings. We aim to offer a unifying theory which outlines the basic philosophies of the approach and what they look like in reality.

The techniques described in this book are compatible with the professional requirements of all those professions listed above, and they can be used to help attain the outcomes in *Every Child Matters* of staying safe, being healthy, enjoying and achieving, making a positive contribution and achieving economic well-being. They also meet the criteria of recent reports which have recommended that universal skills are shared across the children's workforce, including:

- effective communication and engagement
- child and young person development
- safeguarding and promoting the welfare of the child
- supporting transitions
- multi-agency working
- sharing information.

(DCSF 2008)

While specific training requirements in different sectors will inevitably differ, one unifying theme running through all sectors is the importance of listening to the child's voice.

Traditionally our knowledge of child development and accepted ways of working with children has been influenced by psychiatric and psychological knowledge. This is extremely useful, but it is fundamentally problem-based, with children categorized so they can be more easily understood and 'treated' by expert professionals. It can be argued that categorization is helpful; for example, a child diagnosed with attention deficit hyperactivity disorder (ADHD) will then receive the medical intervention that is considered required and to provide an understanding of why a child is behaving in a particular way. However, an alternative argument is that this diagnosis then places the 'problem' within the child, which can lead to the child becoming pathologized. Furthermore, categorization can define and conclude what intervention is best for the individual without considering their own unique ideas and strengths with regards to what would work best for them in the future.

Practice activity

1. Make a list of some of the ways that being labelled as learning disabled could be helpful. Then make a list of some of the ways having a label could be detrimental. It may help to think about how we label other people and things.

2. Consider how, in your role, you can make best use of labels and terminology for all the children you work with, whilst avoiding some of the negative impacts associated with being labelled.

(Jones and Northway 2006, p.785)

Whatever your profession, the best ways of working with children are those in which workers practise alongside children and their families as respected partners in an agreed activity. This approach is applicable to all workforce contexts, from early years through health and well-being, leisure, education and employment, youth and safeguarding and social care. Additionally it needs to be applied whether you are working with individual children, or families, or groups of children, able-bodied or disabled, and whatever intellectual ability.

There are a number of ways of working with children that fulfil all these criteria. For example, narrative approaches have been used in work with whole communities at high risk of diabetes, as well as small groups of children with anorexia (Epston 1998), and the strengths model recognizes and values resilience and resourcefulness (Saleeby 1992; Edwards and Pedrotti 2004). Another approach is focusing on solutions (Berg and Steiner 2003; Myers 2008) – the focus of this book.

Although narrative and strengths perspectives influence our work, we choose to concentrate on solution focused practice. This method was developed from asking people what worked best for them, and keeping all these elements and discarding any others (de Shazer 1985, 1988, 1991). Solution focused practice aims to restore children's problem-solving potential and mobilize their own inner resources or resourcefulness. This we believe to be an appropriate and effective unifying theory and practice for all branches of the children's workforce.

Solution focused practice

A major reason why we promote this way of working is because a central element is how we talk and listen to children. Talking is not a neutral activity; how we talk about events and ourselves has the capacity to change how we are: 'Talk constructs the future and change … the problems are already constructed: what matters is constructing solutions' (Parton and O'Byrne 2000, p.97). Thus how we describe or talk about things, whether these are experiences in general or our interactions with others, provides a specific understanding. Consider the words that you may have heard exchanged between professionals about children and/ or families at both informal and formal settings. On occasions when the descriptions have been pathologizing of that individual, how helpful are these when attempting to move children beyond their problems? If you imagine having a supervisor who constantly focused on things that were not going well in your practice or was critical of your work and never acknowledged your skills and strengths, how would that affect you? The importance is in achieving a balanced perspective so that concerns are not minimized alongside locating people's abilities and qualities to support them in moving forward.

Practice activity ———————————————————

Eleven-year-old Keira has struggled with her academic work since starting secondary school. Her concentration is poor and she easily gives up when faced with any task she finds difficult. She is a popular pupil with a crowd of girlfriends and tends to play to the gallery in class. Yesterday her maths teacher told her to stop messing about and get on with her work. Keira continued talking to other pupils. The teacher went quietly over to her at which point

Keira told her she could stuff her f***ing fractions and stormed out of the room.

1. Words used to describe Keira would probably include: disrespectful, uncooperative, disruptive, defiant and impossible. Think of other words that begin a re-description of Keira that is less pathologizing, but do not minimize concerns.

2. What do you think is the teacher's goal for Keira?

3. What do you think Keira's best hopes might be?

4. How could the teacher talk with Keira in a way that would engage her cooperation?

PROMPT QUESTIONS THE TEACHER COULD ASK HERSELF

- When in class has Keira responded appropriately?
- How did she do this?
- Who else was involved, etc.?
- When else has Keira shown ability?
- How often?
- What do her successes tell me about her abilities?
- How can I share my discoveries of her successes so that she hears what I am saying and is motivated by them?
- How can this begin on a small scale so that Keira can be more successful?

PROMPT QUESTIONS THE TEACHER COULD ASK KEIRA

- What are your best hopes?
- What has worked for you in school that I should know about?
- We have clashed in the past. Let's try, just for today, to work together. Tell me what I can do to help that happen.
- You get on well with the other pupils. What would they say they like about you that makes them want to stay friends with you?
- How can we use these same qualities/skills in the classroom?

Thompson (2003) says that we cannot expect to be successful in our attempts to communicate if we are not able to listen effectively. We examine effective listening more fully in the next chapter but, here, we briefly mention some barriers to effective listening that a problem focus may inadvertently encourage:

- A child may have many features of a recognized problem, such as ADHD or dyslexia, but this does not mean that the child is like *all* children with ADHD or dyslexia.
- Categorizing children has the advantage of making them eligible for extra resources, but it can have the disadvantage of leading you to assume that you know what the problem is and indulging in mind reading.
- Similarly, thinking you know what problem you are dealing with sometimes means that you only listen to the bits you want to hear and then you may filter out much of what the child is saying.
- Equally, being certain that we know what the problem is, and de facto, the solution, means we stop listening.
- Funnily enough, offering advice to children on how to solve their problems closes down effective listening.

Practice activity

The next time someone consults you about a problem (this can be a friend, colleague or child you are working with):

- think what advice you are going to offer but *don't do this yet*
- ask them what they have tried so far, what worked and what didn't
- if something worked a little bit, talk with them about how they can do more of it
- if nothing worked, ask them what they could do differently
- ask if they have any resources for this
- discover what resources outside of themselves they need
- and, if it hasn't already been mentioned as something they tried and it didn't work, forget about the advice you were going to offer.

A fundamental belief of the solution focused approach is the genuine recognition that each person is the 'expert' in their own life and is equipped with the knowledge to know what works for them. This is in contrast to other models where the worker is considered as the expert in 'fixing' the problems. The expertise of a solution focused worker is in structuring conversations to enable children and their families to locate any knowledge, strengths, skills and abilities which will support them in achieving their hopes and wishes. This requires good communication skills and discipline. We emphasize the importance of genuineness too, because workers can learn solution focused techniques but unless there is a sincere belief that those you are working with have the qualities and skills to achieve positive change, then workers may find themselves bringing knowledge and assumptions of understanding the 'problem' with them. Then they are in danger of imposing their own solutions and stifling children's cooperation and creativity.

A further fundamental aspect of the solution focused approach is the appreciation that each child has the ability to identify the situation that they will be in when a problem has stopped happening, or is happening less often enough for it not to be so much of a problem. When the child has constructed what this will look like, this provides clear, concrete child-centred focused goals. Furthermore, these descriptions are best when they are solution-orientated, such as, 'I will be arriving at college on time,' in contrast to descriptions which are an absence of problems, such as, 'I will stop being late.'

We have found when working with schools that goal setting can also be undertaken on a group basis. Jackie has worked closely with schools in increasing levels of respect and safer behaviour within classrooms and schools as a whole. To generate a description of what staff and pupils hope for and to establish clear client-orientated goals, Jackie asked them questions such as:

- What makes a safe classroom?
- What does it look like?
- How is everyone behaving in this safe classroom?
- How are you talking to each other when you are in your safe classroom?

Individual and group strengths are identified so that pupils are supported in maintaining a safe classroom, and they are asked to consider, 'How could you help someone when they need help to remember what is OK and not OK in your safer classroom?'

Once these goals are defined, Jackie begins to locate exceptions, those times when the problems have not happened or happened less, focusing in great detail on where, when, who was involved and how it happened. For example, when pupils tell Jackie that a safe classroom would be one where there isn't any bullying, Jackie would ask:

- When there's no bullying, how will you be behaving instead?
- Can you tell me if any of this is happening already?
- Where does it happen?
- When does it happen?
- Who was doing this?
- How did it happen?
- Can you do more of this?

This sort of conversation can be very powerful and uplifting as it provides children with evidence that they have the resources, strengths and abilities to make the necessary changes in their lives. When children struggle to find times when they have overcome a difficulty that is troubling them or the adults in their lives, you can take a position of curiosity to consider times when the problems have happened less, and then ask scaled questions to build upon this.

As we mentioned earlier, this approach was developed from asking people what worked for them (and discarding what they said doesn't work), therefore it is evidence-based. Its applicability in a wide range of situations and with children of all abilities has been demonstrated in a number of research studies, confirming the evidence-base (for an overview, see Macdonald 2007). We turn now to demonstrate how the philosophy and practice of solution focused approaches link with the philosophy of the Workforce Strategy (DCSF 2008a) and children's views on the sort of work and worker they find most helpful.

From solution focused philosophy to practice

Reaching full potential and providing children with real options and real choice

Solution focused practice is aspirational – it can help to enable children to reach their full potential. In meeting with a child the worker identifies what the child's best hopes and goals are. Where a child is too young to articulate these, the outcomes detailed in *Every Child Matters* (see list on p.9) can provide appropriate goals. Solution focused practice emphasizes the importance of language and advocates a focus on the resources and skills and how these can contribute and assist the person in achieving their goal. As with adults, children are expected to formulate realistic, achievable goals that are not harmful to themselves or others.

Participation – involving children in change

A solution focused approach supports children in the development of their own solutions to problems and difficulties through identifying and exploring those times when the problem or difficulty could have happened but didn't, or the person experienced the problem less. For example, when Jackie worked in youth justice, her conversations with young people who were in trouble for violence or public disorder were about the times when they could have become violent but didn't, searching for exactly what was different on these occasions so that they could learn from these successes in being non-violent. Looking for exceptions is important at any level of behaviour that is unacceptable to adults or other children; for example, a small child will probably respond to a teacher's or parent's concern by promising 'to be good' but may not know how to *do* 'being good' because we are all so much better at telling children what they are doing wrong than we are at noticing what they are doing right.

Practice activity ——————————————

1. Next time you have to speak to a child about his/her behaviour, express your concern about the behaviour briefly and then ask:

   ○ Can you tell me if there have been any times when the behaviour didn't happen (for example, can you tell me when Amy has annoyed you and you didn't hit her?)

- When did this happen?
- Where did it happen?
- How did you do it?
- Was it hard or easy?
- Do you think you can do it again?
- Will you need any help to do it?

2. Next time you are trying to help a child who keeps getting a task wrong, express your concern briefly and then ask:

- Have there been any times when you achieved the task (for example, can you tell me if you ever managed to get all your homework done?) Or
- Can you tell me about any times when you almost managed the task? Or
- Can you tell me about any times when you succeeded in something that was hard when you first had a go? [Then go on to the questions in part 1]

We are not interested in why problems occur, or the nature of problems because we are too busy helping children find their solutions to difficulties. Neither is it necessarily useful to know why; Wittgenstein (1963, 1980) questioned the belief that there was a need to know the root of the problem in order to answer it. This may seem counterintuitive, but from our experience we have often found that children we are working with understand why they behave in a certain way and want support in finding ways to manage their behaviour/problem/difficulty differently. We have also found that children may not wish to, or feel unable to, explore the reasons why they are struggling, but do wish to change things. Digging into the problem, even with the best intentions, would clearly be disrespectful to that child, and possibly painful. You will notice throughout the examples in this book that we never ask a child 'why?' Should a child ask 'why?' we would ask what is most important to them: to have a solution or know why?

Furthermore, as de Shazer (1991) explicitly states, the solution is not necessarily related to the problem. Again this seems to run counter to commonsense, but we find that when we listen very carefully to children and ask them what they think might work, they come up with solutions that have nothing to do with the problem. Neither are they solutions that we would ever have thought of, as Christopher's solution shows.

Case example ──────────────────

Ten-year-old Christopher was a troubled child who wept a lot, talked about dying, pierced his body, wet and soiled, couldn't concentrate on school work, and couldn't cope in the school playground or playing out at home. His parents were terribly worried about his thoughts of death but, when asked which of all these very troubling things bothered him the most, he whispered that he wanted to work on the 'toilet thing' first. Christopher explained that the 'toilet thing' had been making his life a misery since he was four years old. He went to the toilet lots of times each day and sat there for ages. When he managed to pass a motion, he flushed it away but it was very sneaky and 'comes back up and goes up my bum again.' He called this problem PP (for pooh pants). He remembered that he had outwitted it a few times, but wasn't sure how. He thought PP wouldn't like it when he wore his glow pyjamas. He also thought PP liked white toilet paper but might dislike green or peach-coloured paper. He went home to find out how these solutions worked.

At the next session, his mother reported that there had been no soiling at all. Christopher said that the green paper had worked better than the peach paper. (Milner 2001, pp.94–97)

Participation – involving children in multi-agency work

Children experience a sense of empowerment in response to our curiosity and style of conversation. A fundamental principle of solution focused ways of working is the notion of the worker not being responsible for, or the expert in, locating the problem or solution. Instead their responsibilities and expertise lie in constructing a conversation which enables children to find their own solutions. This is more than just following a specific style of questioning. Each worker needs to believe genuinely that the children and their families do know best and are the experts in their own lives. We have found that this approach has been equally effective with children and their families whether they are meeting with us voluntarily or under some form of coercion. There is evidence of correlation between parental involvement and a child's attainment and well-being (DCSF 2008a). The importance of working with families is also evidenced by comments within the child and young person's perspective on integrated working:

- Know me, listen and hear.
- Someone who knows me and my family/carers and talks with us about how things are going.
- They know me as a whole person and talk about my strengths as well as any problems I might have. (DCSF 2008a, Annex C)

As such the importance of workers' engagement with those people who play an important role in a child's life is key. We have found that such engagement, even in difficult situations when concerns are being shared with parents about their ability to keep their children safe, can be achieved when conversations are respectful and transparent.

Transparency

Communication, and specifically how this is undertaken and its relevance and importance, was an issue which stood out from the consultations which were undertaken with children and young people about what they want from the children's workforce. This fits with a central tenet of solution focused practice: the acknowledgement that language is of central importance, because how we talk about something generates a particular understanding of it. We have frequently experienced this within case conferences where the language that is shared between professionals can be both judgemental and pathologizing to children and families. This has a detrimental effect on children's motivation and affects their relationships with those professionals adversely. This is not to be misinterpreted in assuming that when someone has committed a crime or where a child has been hurt that this should not be challenged or addressed; quite the contrary. However, to increase motivation, change and safety there needs to be a balance between identifying concerns alongside occasions when things have been different and better. It is possible to work within a child protection framework and engage in transparent and respectful conversations.

It is clear from the consultation undertaken with children and young people (DCSF 2008a) that children's experiences with workers can either hinder or help further communication and subsequent engagement. White and Bateman (2008) suggest that it is 'Helpful to see engagement as located in various actions which increase in the relationship between people as they get to know each other and learn to value what they have to offer to each other.' (p.18) Such 'actions' would include honest and transparent practice, giving people time and opportunities and as practitioners reflecting on what we could do differently to support and achieve increased levels of engagement.

Finding a way to communicate with children is essential in helping them locate a voice, and ultimately their full participation. This is a very obvious statement, but from discussions with both practitioners and children, locating a language can be difficult. For example, Gavin was 15 years old, but functioned at a very much lower level. He easily became frustrated and his mother hoped he could learn to control his temper better. Gavin certainly didn't want to sit down and talk about his temper, but he was perfectly happy to draw a picture of it, and talk about what his picture meant. Gavin talking about his picture showed that he had a surprisingly good understanding of complex concepts. He not only knew what 'being calm' was like for him (the pale coloured side of his drawing) but he also knew that his temper control would come in steps (the brightly coloured stripy side of his picture).

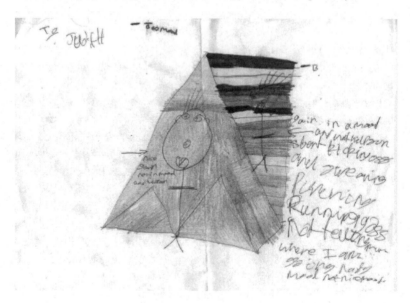

ASSESSMENT

It is also important to acknowledge children's wishes that their strengths be recognized (DCSF 2008a). We find that a consistent emphasis on strengths increases children's motivation to work with us, so on initial contact with families, we enquire about the strengths of each family member. Parents particularly are often taken aback by our interest and curiosity in what they and their children are good at. In a solution focused practice, talk of strengths is important because despite life's struggles, everyone possesses strengths that can be used to improve the quality of their lives. Workers should respect these strengths and the directions in which children wish to apply them: 'When we consider the stresses under which many service users live, we have to be impressed with their ability to keep going, perhaps not all the time, but more often than we give them credit' (Howe 2009, p.101).

Focusing on strengths turns workers away from the temptation to judge or blame children for their difficulties and towards discovering how they have managed to survive, even in the most difficult of circumstances. All environments – even the most bleak – contain resources, maintains Saleeby (2007, p.285). We find that talking about strengths frequently decreases levels of anxiety in children and young people, particularly in situations where a young person has committed an offence and is preparing for an onslaught of negativity from parents and teachers. Instead it becomes an audience to what their parents think they are good at. We are also aware through conversations with parents at the end of our work that engagement has increased due to their experiencing a feeling of empowerment to remain as the experts in their own and children's lives. Government doesn't bring children up, parents do, so there needs to be more constructive support for parents (DCSF 2007a). Parents can experience too much negativity when their children are behaving badly and pass this on to the child by becoming angry and disappointed in them. Judith bypasses this by ending her initial strengths conversation with the comment: 'I don't know what you have been doing with [name of child] but with all these good points you must have been doing something seriously right.' This frees them up to join with the child against the problem, using all the strengths, resources, qualities, skills, etc. which you have discovered.

Practice activity

We invite you to join our anti tut tut club. Next time you are at a supermarket, café, in a queue, etc. steadfastly ignore any temptation to make tut tutting noises or give disapproving looks at any badly behaved child. Instead, look out for well-behaved children and make a point of noticing these with their parents. It is advisable to move swiftly on after paying this compliment as parents are so unused to receiving compliments that they will probably be embarrassed. Hopefully the child will behave beautifully on all subsequent outings to that public place – in the hope that some other adult notices their good behaviour. And that person could be you.

FEEDBACK

Constructive feedback is vital at whatever level of contact with children, be this a certificate of achievement from a class teacher or copies of therapeutic notes. This is not simply about praise, it is about identifying children's competence and sense of being in control of their lives and able to solve their problems. Any sport instructor will tell you that children learn most quickly when they practise their successes and become disheartened when they have to repeat their failed attempts. This is because it increases their motivation, uses their skills, and helps them to work out what they are doing right so that they can do more of it.

SAFEGUARDING

A solution focused approach can also be adopted within a child protection framework and the responsibilities, both to the young person/family you are working with and the wider community, which come with this. Turnell and Edwards (1999) devised a Signs of Safety approach as a comprehensive (risk) assessment which documents both concerns and safety alongside canvassing the goals and perspectives of both professionals and family members. In child protection work the main solution focus is on developing and increasing the level of safety. Thus parents and children are required to demonstrate behaviour which is measurably safe. The way that the assessment is structured enables parents to understand others' concerns alongside an acknowledgement of strengths and positive parenting. This facilitates transparency and an understanding of what needs to be different for professionals to no longer be concerned. For example, workers at Barnardo's The Junction Project in Rotherham for children and young people whose behaviour is sexually concerning or harmful involve the child and family in the risk/safety assessment. After explaining the purpose of the meeting, the worker rolls out a large sheet of paper on the floor and draws (or asks the young person to do this) two columns, one of which is headed 'Concerns' or 'Worries' (depending on the age of the child) and each corresponding safety feature. Thus everyone's concerns are listed and everyone has a clear idea of what will be different when there is sufficient safety. Strengths are identified as resources to create more safety for vulnerable children. The worker will then begin to document things that they have already heard as well as asking questions such as, 'Since the behaviour came to light, what have you done differently to increase safety?'

The information that is shared (in response to these questions) is noted down in the other column headed 'Safety'. As these questions are asked and there is a recognition from families that we are not going to blame, or *tell* them what they need to be doing, but rather intend on building on the levels of safety that are already visible, there is a noticeable difference in their motivation to engage with the worker and the process, alongside a reduction in feelings of anxiety. We are clear from the outset that if we have any concerns about the welfare of their own or other children that this information will be shared with the local authority. For example, where there are few, or no, signs of safety, concern is obviously increased.

Case example

Steven, a 14-year-old, was referred to the service after he had been discovered to have been touching a young family friend inappropriately. On visiting the family for the first time, Jackie found Steven to be verbally abusive and clearly unhappy with her presence. He quickly left the room. His mum and sisters began to share stories about Steven's difficult behaviour. After 15 minutes of listening to their problem talk, Jackie acknowledged the family's recent difficulties and documented their specific concerns. She then asked permission to hear about times when things had gone well, times when Steven had shown responsibility, trust and helpfulness. She also asked his mum what stood out about her children that made her proud as a parent. In response to these questions Jackie began to hear about recent times when Steven had helped around the house, tided his room without being asked, gone to school regularly and on time, and shown a caring manner towards his niece. During this conversation, Jackie was aware that Steven was sitting at the top of the stairs. By the end of the visit he was sitting on the bottom step. Jackie wrote to Steven later, sharing with him the responsibilities, strengths and qualities that she heard from his family. On her next visit Steven agreed to speak with her and begin work on safety building.

Part of this Signs of Safety assessment is also to enquire about the goals of the young person, family and any professionals involved. Families find it helpful to have a clear understanding of what needs to be different for professionals to cease their intervention. The final part is to ascertain other people's views of the young person's ability to take control of the sexual behaviour. This is done by asking scaled questions; for example, 'If 1 means you have no control over your sexually inappropriate behaviour and 10 means you have full control, where are you on this scale today?' Also, 'Where would your [any concerned person's name] put you on the scale?' Alongside the canvassing of individual views, the use of scaled questions generates increased conversation about progress and levels of safety. For example, 'So you say you are at 7. What are you doing, what have people noticed differently about you that puts you at 7?' Thus the child has to provide evidence to support an assertion that progress in safety building is being achieved. A follow-on question could be, 'What will be happening when you are one point higher?' When a scale is reviewed and the position is lower, a question can be asked such as, 'So you say it's only 5 today, what safety is still around that has stopped you being a 4?' and 'What needs to be happening to get you back to a 7?' Such future-orientated conversations enable children and young people to consider the steps and subsequent plans that are required. Remaining focused on future safety avoids the worker getting embroiled in why something has happened and generating feelings of blame and failure.

Key points

- Solution focused practice is especially appropriate for the children's workforce because it is strengths-based, participatory and transparent and, above all, it is fundamentally ambitious for every child.
- The philosophy underpinning solution focused practice includes an unwavering belief in children's capacities to find their own solutions – the guiding principle is if it works, do more of it. If it doesn't work, do something different.
- The techniques provide a discipline within which the worker can remain true to the philosophy and principle. It has been found to work equally well with problems such as anorexia, violence, substance misuse and mental illnesses, regardless of learning ability, and with long lasting results (Macdonald 2007, Chapter 6).

The key points of solution focused practice are:

- Don't trust your own theories about anyone; remain *curious* about how they are different.
- Do believe that people already know what they can do and are able to do it – it's just that sometimes they don't realize this. Help them to see it by asking helpful questions.
- The problem is the problem; get the children and their families working against it with you.
- It's not a problem if it has no solution (at least it is not a problem to be changed, only to be coped with).
- We don't need to understand the problem in order to understand the solution, unless it is a purely physical matter or a question of medication.
- Don't worry about people resisting change – encourage them to resist the problem.
- Use lots of scaled questions, with $10 =$ perfect and $1 =$ the pits.
- Don't take too much responsibility. Responsibility is like a cake – the more you eat the less there is for the other person. Your responsibility mainly includes asking questions that invite them to take more of the cake.

- There is always something about everyone that is okay; spend some time thinking about what that is, because it can fix what is not okay. No problem is ever 100 per cent bad always, so talk about *exceptions* to problems.

- Rather than looking for more understanding of the problem, look instead at what people are *doing well*.

- Slow down – go back to what the person hopes for (has any of that ever happened before? What coping strategies worked in the past?). The more time you spend on their strengths and successes the better. Compliment them on coping *in spite of* all they have to endure.

- Remember that a solution may well not be related to a problem.

- Avoid negativity by not asking a question to which you know the answer, i.e. don't ask 'How are you?' if you know the answer will be, 'Awful.' Instead, ask 'What's better since we last met?' If the answer is 'Nothing,' ask 'What was better just after we met?,' 'What was better the next day?,' 'What was better this morning?' This conveys that you are more interested in what is better than in what is worse or the same.

- We can make a possibility more possible by talking, imagining and figuring out how to start it. This means talking in detail about what it will be like, what the child will be doing, how the child will feel, what other people will notice, etc. (Milner and O'Byrne 2002).

We address each one of these key points in more detail in the subsequent chapters.

Chapter Two

Taking Children Seriously

This chapter looks at the first, and possibly the most important, skill needed in working with children: effective communication and engagement. In other words, getting off to a good start. Underpinning all solution focused practice with children is the basic principle of taking children seriously as people, respecting them in their own right. This is not as self-evident as it sounds. Professionals talk about the importance of being child-centred; of engaging with children to build up a relationship; of needing a sound understanding of child development; and, of being respectful. However, if you look at what children say about the workers who are helping them you soon find out that children have their own ideas about what these terms mean to them (DoH 2000, p.45; DCSF 2008a).

Being child-centred

It is very hard for any adult to be truly child-centred, simply because they are adult. They listen to children, consult them and sometimes invite them to meetings, but they mostly do this *selectively*. This is an unconscious process based on the requirements, procedures and service arrangements of their employing organizations (Gill and Jack 2007, p.53).

These requirements do not take into account the difficulties in implementing them. Being child-centred is not only considered desirable, but it is actually prescribed in that all professionals must take into account first and foremost the best interests of the child. However, Mullender (1999a) considers this to be a suspiciously catch-all phrase which does little to spell out what each individual child's needs are. She adds that despite a plethora of available psychological research findings about children's developmental needs, this 'does not have the capacity to predict anything about any individual child' (Mullender 1999b, p.11). The Child and Adolescent Mental Health Services (CAMHS) strategy (DoH 2008) suggests that professionals should understand child development, *and* provide each child with a package of individualized care, although interventions based on an understanding of overall child development are not necessarily individualized.

Obviously you need sufficient knowledge about child development so that you can tailor your conversations with children according to their age and aptitude, and to assess whether or not they are meeting expected development milestones. But there is a danger in assuming that all children are doing is 'developing'.

Taylor (2004) argues that viewing children as preparing for adulthood rather than viewing them as people in their own right, living their lives and accomplishing in the here and now, means that their capacities for understanding and reasoning can be underestimated, and they can be deemed incompetent to make decisions. This can lead to their being misunderstood.

As adults, we naturally look at things from an adult perspective so when we talk with children we are looking at how they relate to us and we are filtering what they tell us through our favourite theories and knowledge. These are most likely to be concerned with long-term dangers to health (such as smoking and substance misuse), and welfare (such as pregnancy and teenage delinquency). Children of course, look at things from a child's perspective and are much more concerned with their everyday relationships with other children, being safe from harm (e.g., cyber bullying) and humiliation (such as being shown up), and having a laugh.

Engaging with children

How best to communicate with children has been largely influenced by the counselling literature in which it is axiomatic that children are only truly engaged through the development of a therapeutic relationship and that this relationship will:

- take time to develop
- probably be resisted
- include the child saying things that are not necessarily what they mean and
- involve gentle interpretative challenges.

Many adults undergoing counselling will find this interpretive challenging very helpful, and those who are not so psychologically minded can always opt out of the counselling or shop around for another counsellor. Children don't have this option. We have met children undergoing psychotherapy whose protests that they 'don't want to do it any more' have been ignored on the grounds that their 'resistance' is not only to be expected, but also a sign that progress is being made. The problem with this is that the adult becomes the expert on what is going on in the child's mind and world more generally. And it is only too easy to get it completely wrong.

Case example

> Simon attempted to hang himself when his parents separated, and was receiving psychiatric in-patient treatment. His school referred him for counselling three years later after he fell out with a friend and told a teacher that he wished he had never been born. His teachers were worried that he would attempt suicide again, fears that were fuelled by an 'interpretation' of his black spiky handwriting with many crossings out as indicative of 'suicidal ideation'. Talking with Simon revealed that other pupils were teasing him because of his psychiatric history – they called him 'hangman'. He explained his black spiky handwriting as the consequence of missing learning how to do joined-up writing at his old school (he was a psychiatric in-patient at the time) and he tended to make many mistakes when rushed. His solution was to put his hand to his neck in a pretend pull the next time he was called 'hangman' (the taunts quickly stopped) and to use Tippex to cover his crossings out. (Milner 2001, pp.131–132)

Where young children express themselves indirectly through play there are even more opportunities for misunderstanding. The worker becomes even more expert so this sort of work with children is seen as different from, and rather more special than, the sort of play that is encouraged in nurseries. Oddly enough it is often called *direct* work with children, even though its aim is to work with the indirect communications of children. Central to this expertise is the idea that the therapeutic relationship is where change happens. The danger here is that the child's real world of relationships with family and friends is marginalized. This is an enormous waste of vital resources as well as adding a tremendous burden on the adult to fix everything.

As we saw in the previous chapter, solution focused practice is very different:

- It does not assume that engaging children is difficult (Berg and Steiner 2003).

- It does not try to replace important people in children's lives. Instead it recruits them as important members of the child's helping team (Barnardo's, undated).

- It does not worry about resistance. In solution focused practice, resistance is considered to be just that: a protest that tells us that we haven't yet found out how they wish to be supported, so we must discover their unique way of cooperating.

- It does not assume that the relationship will necessarily be lengthy; instead it views the relationship as short term and transitional until its purpose is fulfilled.

- The relationship must be transparent and genuinely two way.

Respecting children

Children tell us very clearly how they wish to be treated by adults. They want us to listen carefully, without trivializing; be available and accessible, with regular and predictable contact; accepting, explaining and suggesting options and choices; to be realistic, reliable and straight talking; and be trustworthy in terms of confidentiality and consulting with them before taking action (DoH 2000, p.45; McNeish, Newman and Roberts 2002). Almost ten years later, government consulted with children again and they said more or the less the same things (DoH 2008). It is clear from this that it doesn't matter how accurate your empathy is if you are not punctual, reliable, courteous and trustworthy. We would add that we consider it important that you are clean and tidy too; it's disrespectful to assume that children aren't bothered how you look. Attending to these basics shows children that you are taking them seriously. It is especially important when you are working with children whose behaviour is disrespectful as they are very often treated with disrespect at the same time as they are being told to be more respectful. Children also tell us that they want us to explain ourselves to them. They don't always know why we are talking to them (DoH 2008, 1.2).

Explaining yourself

If conversations with children are to be useful, children need to know what is the purpose of them. They need to know what we can and cannot do, when and where we will do it, what our and other adults' concerns are, details of any rules and boundaries, how long it is likely to take, and where we can be contacted. For example, swimming instructors explain which strokes they will help the children learn but that they won't be doing any diving (being realistic about their role); details of when and where lessons will take place (punctuality, regular and predictable contact); whether or not children will be wearing flotation devices or staying in the shallow end (keeping children safe); where they can get dry and how much time there is to dress and undress (privacy and ensuring children are not embarrassed); they encourage children when they get it right (facilitating learning), and so on. As Jackie and Judith are involved with children with complex problems, who may well be worried or resentful about meeting with us, we take even more care to explain the solution focused process and ourselves:

> *Hello, my name is Jackie. The way that I work with families is by focusing on solutions more than problems. This means that I will ask you some questions around how you will know that our work together has been useful and/or what would you like to be different as a result of you meeting with me. When you have decided, we will then look at times when this has happened/is happening and what you did/do to enable this.*
>
> *So you will notice that I like to talk about solutions, what life will be like when it has worked out well for you. I don't usually talk much about problems except when it's helpful. So, when we are talking, we can talk about problems if you want to, but you don't have to. I do have a couple of rules: one is that it's okay for you to leave the room at any time if you want a break, another is that when you are out of the room, other people are only allowed to say good stuff about you. If I ask you a question you don't want to answer, please don't look down at your hands because I'll be too busy writing down what you say so I can send you some notes later to notice. Just tell me to mind my own business. Or, if you are a really polite sort of person, perhaps you could say something like 'pass'. Which would be best for you? So, can you tell me what will be different in your life when everything has worked out for you/ the problem has gone/etc.?*

Then we would check that the information we had been given on the child was accurate. We have found these conversations helpful as they encourage transparency and put the work in a context. Furthermore, we hope that on a longer term basis that this will provide another way that children and their families can think and respond to difficulties outside our work with them, as well as shifting their own family conversations to consider each other's strengths as an alternative to recognizing each other's weaknesses. We have witnessed the dramatic change that this can have on children and families and at times how quickly this can occur.

Case example

Jackie went to visit a family where 14-year-old Sarah had inappropriately touched her younger brother. Inevitably there was a lot of pain and upset, alongside very mixed feelings towards Sarah. At the beginning of the visit Jackie simply sat and listened as the family offloaded some very strong negative feelings about their daughter. This was not only in relation to the recently displayed behaviour, but also her general behaviour and attitude at both home and school. After a while Jackie began to gently interject by asking questions about what Sarah did that made them feel like proud parents, what skills they had as parents and specific times that Sarah had shown responsible and caring behaviour. The parents were quite open in that they found these questions difficult, which was acknowledged, alongside voicing their surprise that Jackie was interested in their strengths as parents, as generally they were being given the impression by other professionals that they were useless and failing as parents. Jackie explained that whilst it was important not to forget or be dismissive about the reasons which had brought them to be working together, it is equally important, when thinking about increasing future safety, that we have conversations which focus on times that safe behaviour has been present in the past and the individual and family strengths and abilities that have been present to enable this to happen. This identification will then make those competences more transparent.

At the next session, Sarah's mother asked if she could have a few words with Jackie. She then brought out a list which outlined eight constructive things that Sarah had done since they had last met. This is not something which Jackie had asked the family to do and, therefore, confirmed to her the validity and usefulness of taking time to explain the process of the work and specifically how the work was going to be undertaken. Following this experience, Jackie now frequently asks families, teachers, social workers, etc. to actually document times that abilities, strengths, etc. are displayed.

Another way that we have found helpful in facilitating strength-based conversation at the beginning (and throughout) the work, is using Strengths cards (info@innovativeresources.org). This is a pack of colourful picture cards which have a particular quality written on each one, for example, patient, organized, caring, etc. The cards can be introduced in an individual session or incorporated in a family or group session whereby you ask individuals to pick those (or limit it to say one or two) that they think represent themselves, or ask one family member to pick another. It is important to get a rich description of how a particular strength has been displayed. We have had the privilege of hearing some lovely conversations between family members, as well as witnessing the positive impact this has had on children and their families when they come to recognize that their contributions and efforts are noticed. Some children, especially those who have been heavily criticized for their behaviour, can find this difficult to do, so it is important to go slowly to prevent putting them under further pressure. Equally, families in difficulty can struggle to see the 'good stuff', which is another reason to limit the number of cards to one or two at the beginning and build it up to maybe half a dozen as families become fully fledged skill spotters!

Where you are talking with children makes some difference, but not a lot. You don't necessarily need a special room with lots of toys and activities. Many of you will find that you are talking with children in chaotic homes, classrooms, sometimes on the street. A group of well-child nurses even held solution focused telephone conversations with families unable to attend their clinic (Polaschek and Polaschek 2007). You don't necessarily need to take people off to a quiet room; it is perfectly possible to have a useful conversation with them in any of these environments. Even when you are in a quiet room with a child, they may well feel more comfortable talking to you standing up, or from the other end of the room, or from the staircase. None of this matters as long as you treat the child with respect and put your own ideas to one side so that you can show genuine curiosity. Whatever 'tools' you may need, for example, paper and colouring pens for children who prefer to communicate through drawing and writing, can all be carried in a sturdy bag. When you are dealing with a large group of people, such as in a classroom, or a busy family home, it is helpful to let children know how to signal when they want to talk with you one-to-one. One teacher we know asks her pupils to put their reading books on her chair so that she will know to talk them as soon as she has time. For parents who may well be busy preparing a meal or emptying the washing machine when a child wishes to talk with them, we suggest a secret sign, such as moving an ornament slightly. Should you take a child out to the park or for a meal, it is important that they know you have a purpose and that you are not simply providing a treat. Workers don't always remember to do all these things, as you can see below:

Case example

When Lola was nine, social services became involved as part of a clampdown on unofficial fostering – and a long legal wrangle over Lola's future began.

> A white social worker called Rosie came to see us, and somehow I could tell that mum couldn't stand her. I was too young to understand the significance of her visits. She took me to McDonalds, which I thought was really exciting. One day, as I sucked on a milkshake, Rosie leaned forward and said, 'Wouldn't you like to be with a nice *black* family?' I remember telling her that I had a family already. But she said, 'We are going to find a new family for you. What would you like that family to be like?' I remember telling her that I wanted a dad with a briefcase, and a house with a swimming pool. I had absolutely no idea of the significance of what was happening. I vaguely knew of a court case, and I could tell mum was upset about something, but had no idea that my whole life was going to be turned upside down. (Cable 2009)

Practice activity

- Make a list of all the things Rosie has forgotten to do.
- How would you go about explaining your role to Lola?
- Where would you decide to hold your meetings with Lola?

- How do you think Lola's foster mum felt about Lola being taken off for private talks?

Problem-free talk

If, as solution focused practitioners, we believe that children have the ability to find their own solutions to problems, then we must also be clear about how we will set about finding out how children will 'do' their solutions. Unlike problem-solving approaches where the professional already has the answer, it is quite possible that a child doesn't yet know that they have a solution. After all, children are not consulted very often, and asked for advice even more rarely. Solution focused practice is ambitious for children, so it is important to set each child up to succeed by engaging with them as people, not as problems. We ask about their hobbies, interests, hopes, aspirations, what they enjoy doing, what are they good at, what the hardest thing they have even done is, and so on. This is not idle chit chat; we are genuinely curious to learn more about the person we are talking to. When children tell us things such as that they keep budgies or enjoy going to dance class, we may ask more curious questions, such as:

- Do budgies take a lot of looking after?
- What do you feed them on?
- Do you do all the budgie care?
- Do you care for them on your own?
- What's the best bit of budgie care?
- How did you get to be so good at budgie care?
- Have you always been good at taking responsibility?

What we are trying to do in these sorts of conversations is find out about the personal qualities of the child. This is not the same as looking for positives; it is about identifying and highlighting the child's abilities, competences and skills. As you can see from the example above, being competent in budgie care is a transferable skill as it requires several qualities of a person: kindness, tenderness, responsibility taking, carefulness, reliability, and so on. Once a person's competences are noticed, it is easier to get a solution going.

Practice activity ——————————————————————

Next time you have a conversation with a child you know well, pretend that you have just met them and are curious to find out all about them. Ask lots of questions (dependent on the age of the child) such as:

- What is the hardest thing you have ever done?
- If your pet could talk, what would it tell me about you?
- If you could borrow someone's life for the day, who would it be?
- What good thing do you do that no-one has noticed?
- What was the best time you ever had?

Curious listening

We all know that good communicators listen carefully. Communications literature has much to say on how to listen and give feedback but not much on what adults are supposed to be listening *to* when they hold conversations with children. We sometimes play a game called Respect Bingo (@Mar*co Products, Inc., www.marcoproducts.com) with families, and rarely do the adults win. This is because as adults we believe we know better than children so we often interrupt them, tell them what they are thinking, what they 'really' mean, and what they should be doing: 'We have all been accused of failing to listen to our nearest and dearest. Those less nearly related may be too polite and fail to correct us when we need it most' (Ross 1996, p.92). We find it odd that adults who are in charge of the agenda for the conversation then talk about listening with a 'third ear' for what the child might be trying to convey by their body language or through play.

Solution focused practice makes no effort to listen for what is not being said on the grounds that there may well be nothing to read between the lines. Instead we listen carefully at the level of the word by:

- noting idiosyncratic use of language, repeated words, language that sticks out
- inquiring about any word or phrase that appears to have special meaning for the child
- checking with the child that we have the same meaning of the word and/or picture used. This is especially important when they have picked up formal language from professionals, such as 'appropriate behaviour'

- not changing the words children use in our conversations or reports, making sure that the conversation is developing from the child's words, not our own
- only asking questions to which we do not think we know the answer
- listening to the reply to one question before deciding what our next question is going to be
- asking the child if we are asking questions that are interesting/relevant to them
- asking the child if there are any questions we haven't asked that are important to them.

This is not to say that we don't have an adult agenda; we do, but we are clear and transparent about what our hopes are for the work. In the case of child protection work, we need to see what is happening for us to be confident that safety has increased, and that we don't need to work together any more so that we can recommend closing the case. We are listening for children's skills, competences, abilities, strengths and resiliences because these are the qualities that will be used in the solution. Children like this type of conversation, making it much easier to engage their attention and cooperation.

There also some things we deliberately don't do when we hold conversations with children. We don't:

- interpret what they are saying or check what they are saying against a favourite theory
- ask 'why'; if children knew why they were doing something, they either wouldn't do it or would be embarrassed to admit they did
- use questionnaires or worksheets. These not only constrict the limits of the conversation, but also children tell us that they don't like doing them.

USING HUMOUR AND PLAYFULNESS

Problems have a knack of convincing adults that it's time to get down to the serious business of problem-solving. This approach, say Freeman, Epston and Lobouits (1997) is a way of problem-solving that is familiar to adults, but may well alienate or exclude children and work to the advantage of the problem. This approach also has the danger of making the child *the problem* rather than seeing the child as someone *with a problem*. Even play therapy can become a solemn matter. Freeman *et al.* much prefer a playful approach to serious problems:

> *Like the twin masks of comedy and tragedy, play reflects both the mirth and pathos of human experience. When children and adults meet, play provides a common language to express the breadth and depth of thoughts, emotions, and experience – in this way we share a lingua franca. Moreover, playful communication isn't totally dependent on cognitive development, having the capacity of being highly contagious and inclusive of all ages. (Freeman et al. 1997, p.4)*

Being playful means using humour as a means of engaging people – sharing laughter is a much quicker way of connecting with a child than is establishing 'accurate empathy' – as long as it 'is humour that builds people up, reduces hierarchy or makes the problem look small and ridiculous' (Sharry, Madden and Darmody 2001, p.34).

Case example

Noel missed a lot of school due to illness and found it difficult to return when he was well. His school had been sympathetic to his difficulties and devised a re-introduction programme that involved him attending school mornings only. He was now refusing to go to school at all, spending most of his time in bed. Now 14 and approaching serious GCSE study, his mother was desperate. On arrival, she complained bitterly that Noel was just stubborn as he had messed up the planned gradual reintroduction programme by refusing to go to school mornings only but turning up some afternoons.

Judith replied to his mother, 'So Noel *can* go to school but he prefers to do this when it suits him. I wonder how the teachers handled it when he turned up in the afternoon?' She glanced across at Noel and they both started laughing at the ludicrous situation of Noel deliberately turning up at the 'wrong time'. Gradually the problem began to look ridiculous as Judith and Noel continued to laugh at it. 'Staying in bed' became part of the joke, with Judith suggesting to his mother that this meant she always knew where Noel was and didn't have to worry about him going on the streets and getting into trouble. And how easy it would be to buy Christmas presents for him because all he would need would be some new pyjamas. Mum didn't think this anywhere near as funny as Judith and Noel did, but she went along with it because, for the first time, Noel was enjoying talking about the problem. He went back to school the next day and stayed there. Mum didn't believe it would last so Judith let her book lots of follow-up appointments, and then cancel them.

ALLOWING RISK AND RESPONSIBILITY TAKING

Safeguarding and promoting the welfare of children isn't just about adults keeping children safe from dangerous people and activities. It is also about helping children recognize risks and manage them so that they grow in confidence. This means not being the person with all the answers. For example, although adults are needed to create an environment where young children can play safely, it is important that they are able to facilitate child-led play:

> *Let them take the lead. Children create wonderful things the minute you stop giving them templates. Independent, or child-led, play boosts that feeling of 'I can'. It encourages them to question (what I can do and use to create the effect I need), to have a go and then, as their confidence grows, to move forward to more challenging resources. (Stephanie Mathivet, Pre-school Learning Alliance, quoted in McKibben 2009, p.8)*

The feeling of confidence in growing competence is essential if children are to learn to solve their own problems, with the support of adults where necessary.

There are some situations where adults are not able to safeguard children, situations where children are sometimes more knowledgeable, such as internet use. The Byron Review on internet use (DCSF 2008b) consulted children on how they can enjoy the internet safely. One finding was that children often know about the tools already there to help manage what is seen on the internet and how it is used, but that their parents don't know how to set these up, or if they do, children get round them easily, so it's the adults who need most help here (DCSF 2008b, p.8). In consulting children for this review, Tanya Byron offered children several ways of joining in a useful conversation with her – as well as the usual discussion groups, she invited children to write to her via her blogs. She then invited them to a huge conference and wrote up a summary of her results especially for children. Writing down what children tell you and letting them have written feedback, using their own words, is an important part of taking children seriously.

Another situation where adults feel helpless to safeguard children is where peer group pressure is a major influence, such as substance misuse or sexual risk taking. Any attempt at gaining control, such as grounding the child or saying who they can and cannot have as friends, tends not to work very well. The adult may issue dire warnings, but this is not a particularly effective way of engaging children. Couzens says, 'How to talk about drugs and alcohol needs thoughtfulness. There's often this concept that everything about drugs and alcohol is negative. It's pretty hard to have an interesting conversation if everything is negative!' (Couzens 1999, p.26). However, you can have an interesting conversation about safety and responsibility taking, such as:

- When you go out drinking at the weekend with your mates, how will I know that you will be all right?
- What can you do, and what can I do, to help me understand that you will be all right?
- What are the things that make you know you are going to be all right?
- Could you tell me about them? I might feel a whole lot safer about it if I knew those things?

These questions can be varied for a wide variety of risk-taking situations, such as taking responsibility for physical health (Whiting 2006), and sexual health (Myers and Milner 2007).

Practice activity

Think of a child or young person you are working with whose risky behaviour worries you; for example, a young person who puts their diabetic control at risk by neglecting to inject themselves, or a foster child who sleeps out. Make a list of the questions and advice you have offered in the past. Keep only those that worked well (don't worry if none of them worked; ignoring advice is what young people do). Now, devise a set of safety questions that are appropriate to your work setting.

We have found that young people are able to devise a safety strategy that will minimize the risks they are taking. For example, the girls' group Judith worked with (Milner 2004) came up with a plan that included ordering a taxi from a reputable firm before setting out for the evening; only going to the toilet in pairs; and ensuring they had sufficient credit on their mobile phones so that they could ring each other for support.

Children who can't or won't talk

If you work with children with little or no speech you are probably already experienced in the use of aids such as talking mats (Brewster 2004). Where the children you work with have learning difficulties, you will probably have adapted your programmes to suit their abilities (see for example, Harper and Hopkinson 2002). However, you don't necessarily have to have specialist knowledge to enable you to talk with a child who lacks speech. Adapting a technique described by Iveson (1990), we simply ask other family members, or other children in the class or group, 'if [child's name] could speak, and I were to ask her to choose someone to speak for her, who do you think she would choose?' After some discussion, agreement is usually reached on who understands the child best and can speak for them. If the child has any way at all of communicating, such as nodding, we then ask the child if the others have chosen the right person to represent them. And then we interview that person as the other. This can get confusing in situations where the child representing the one without speech also has something to say on their own account. Here we make it clear which of them we are speaking to by using their different names at the beginning of each question or comment we make.

Asking one person to speak for another also works with children who are either too embarrassed to talk to you or just don't like talking. We ask the child to change places with another person in the room, preferably the person who is most concerned about them, and then interview that person as the child. The child is given two pieces of paper on which is written CORRECT! and WRONG! to hold up after each answer. To make sure that people stay in role, we begin by asking questions in a deliberately serious tone of voice, prefaced by the child's name.

Case example

Darren's mum has brought him for help with his 'inability to control his temper' and 'communication difficulties'. The latter turned out to consist of not talking to adults at all, but he still had a conversation:

Judith: [to mum as Darren] Tell me, Darren, how long has the temper been in you?

Mum: [as Darren] About 12 months. CORRECT!

Judith: [to mum as Darren] So Darren, is it worse or better at the moment?

Mum: [as Darren] It's not as frequent. CORRECT!

Judith: [to mum as Darren] Are the episodes as bad as previously?

Mum: [forgetting her role as Darren] He's only had one really bad one. [Darren has difficulty deciding which paper to hold up, eventually proferring both].

Judith: [to Darren] Is mum doing you well, Darren? [he nods].

Judith: [to mum as Darren] What is the temper like?

Mum: [as Darren] Like a volcano. Exploding! CORRECT!

Judith: [to mum as Darren] Is it a slow or sudden volcano?

Mum: [as Darren] Sudden. CORRECT!

Judith: [to mum as Darren] What does it make you do?

Mum: [as Darren] I don't know. [as herself] Here, Darren, you'll have to speak for yourself. [she changes places with him and takes the two papers]

Judith: [to Darren] What does the temper make you do?

Darren: I don't know.

Judith: Have you got it blocked out?

Darren: No.

Judith: Does the temper make you throw things?

Darren: No.

Judith: Does it make you hit people?

Darren: Yes.

Judith: Does it make you use your fists?

Darren: Yes.

Judith: Does it make you kick?

Darren: Yes.

Judith: Does it make you swear?

Darren: No. [Mum suddenly remembering that she has the right and wrong paper] WRONG!

Judith: Does it make you use the 'f' word?

Darren: No. WRONG!

Judith: The 'b' word?

Darren: No. CORRECT!

Judith: The 'c' word?

Darren: NO! CORRECT!

Judith: Shout?

Darren: No. WRONG!

Judith: Stamp about?

Darren: No. CORRECT!

Judith: Break things?

Darren: No. CORRECT!

By this time both Darren and his mum were laughing and thoroughly enjoying the game and it was possible to talk with Darren about how much control he thought an 11-year-old should have over his temper, and his mum about what made her proud of her son. (For more details, see Milner 2001, pp.139–140.)

Children enjoy hearing their parent addressed by their name and don't hesitate to tell them when they have got an answer wrong. Knowing that they are about to be judged right or wrong tends to make the parent think carefully before answering. When the parents-as-children are getting all their answers right, it is useful to ask a neutral question to see if the child will rate an answer as wrong or elaborate on it. This is especially important where you are concerned that one parent may be influencing the child because the child is afraid, or reluctant to upset that parent. Lewis' father had been getting his 'Lewis' answers right but, as you can see from the following brief extract, Lewis was able to contradict his father.

Case example

Judith: [to dad as Lewis] Tell me 'Lewis', what are the chances of you getting a dog?

Dad: [as Lewis] Pretty non-existent.

Lewis: I wouldn't use those words but at this time none, but maybe when I'm a bit older I'll have a dog.

Another way to check on whether or not a parent is unduly influencing a child is to add a third dimension. In the problem-free talk with Lewis and his sister, Katie, they both talked about enjoying the television programme *Strictly Come Dancing* and had been practising the tango. As they were sitting in a row on the sofa with their father, Judith gave them a pen each to act as microphones and then suggested interviewing them on *Strictly Come Dancing 2* (the follow-up programme where contestants and dancers discuss the weekend show). Lewis chose to be Bruno (a generous judge who frequently awards 10 out of 10) and Katie chose to be Ola (a professional dancer) on the grounds that she could remember her name. They thought dad could be Len, but as this was a head judge role and Judith was attempting to reduce adult influence, she asked him to be Vincent (a professional dancer). Both children were highly amused and showed dad how Vincent signals that he's good looking. After a warm-up question to 'Ola' about 'last night's show', and a brief break while dad fetched larger pens to act as microphones, Judith commented to 'Ola' that there had been a lot in the Sunday papers about how she lived with her dad, but didn't see her mum and that the viewers were just as interested in her personal life as her dancing so maybe she might like to tell them more about how she feels about not seeing her mum. Doing the 'interview' at a fast pace left no time for Katie to second guess what dad might like her to say. Being playful in this way encourages children to be creative in their conversations with adults. For example, one seven-year-old added two more pieces of paper so that as well as CORRECT! and WRONG! he also had AHEM! and a big question mark.

When a child is very young and possibly has divided loyalties, we sometimes begin a conversation with an adult in the hope that the child will join in.

Case example

Three-year-old Taylor has lived with her mum, Cheryl, since her parents divorced. She spends Saturdays with her dad, Martin, and his family. He would like her to have some sleepovers and Taylor had expressed a willingness for these, but Cheryl complains that Taylor comes back from contact in an upset state and has said she doesn't want to sleep over at dad's house. Taylor clung to her mum and nodded her head when mum said this. As Judith talked more with mum, Taylor fetched a catalogue and showed Judith a picture of a bed set she has chosen for her bedrooms in both homes. Judith then visited Taylor at Martin's home, where she found her engrossed in an elaborate game with various dolls and prams. Both grandparents were on the floor playing with her.

Judith: Hello again, Taylor. Do you know what I'm doing here? [Taylor looks up from her game and nods] It's to do with working out when it will be right for you to spend more time with dad.

Taylor: I don't talk about that. [she continues playing her game, steadfastly ignoring attempts to engage her attention through neutral questions about the dolls]

Judith: [to Martin] Which adult here is Taylor most likely to talk with more openly?

Martin: I'd say my mum.

Judith: [to grandma] This is a lovely big house. Do you have a lot of bedrooms?

Grandma: There's four upstairs and one downstairs.

Judith: So, lots of room for everyone. Have you thought where Taylor will sleep if she decides she wants to sleep over?

Grandma: She's already chosen her room. It's the small one upstairs, next to her dad's bedroom.

Judith: I wonder what it would be like if Taylor had a sleepover?

Grandma: It would be like a proper family weekend. With this every other Saturday arrangement, we're practically queueing up to play with Taylor. With more time we could have a Sunday lunch and then spend the afternoon in the garden. Or have a little outing.

Grandad: It would be more normal. We'd do more normal things.

Taylor: [leaving her game and coming to the sofa where Judith and grandma are sitting] I have choosed the paint for my bedroom. It's pink.

Grandma: And she's chosen the decorations. It's nearly ready.

Judith: How exciting. [to Taylor] Would you show it to me?

Taylor: Yes. And the first time I sleep over, granddad says we can go to the seaside.

Children who disrupt conversations

Children can also talk too much, or off the point, or at inappropriate times. One way to handle this is to adapt rules from children's favourite sporting situations. Couzens (1999) describes how he uses Australian football rules in his group sessions with young aboriginal boys:

> *Each week, one student is the designated umpire. If one of the kids breaks one of the ground rules (which have been established by the group) then the umpire gives the student a warning. For a second break of the rules the student is sent off – benched, in the sin bin, for ten or so minutes. The group decides the time. When they come back into the group and apologize, we talk about what happened, what made him feel angry or what sort of sparked him off. If there's a third breakage of the rules then the student has a meeting with the Aboriginal Education Workers, myself, and the principal. But this hardly ever needs to happen. We develop a team game sort of feel and it works fantastically. (Couzens 1999, pp.24–22)*

Another way we have found works well is to ask the disruptive child to 'come to the diary room' (as in *Big Brother*). The 'diary room' doesn't have to be a separate room, it can be any corner of the room in which the group is meeting, because the aim is simply to give the child a chance to explain their behaviour, agree penalties, and settle themselves down before they return to the main group. The group can take it in turns to be 'Big Brother' – they usually adopt a very serious tone – and it is helpful to end the 'diary room' session by asking the child why people should vote for them to stay in the 'Big Brother' house. This enables the child to remember their strengths and good qualities which you are hoping they will put to good use.

Key points

We consider it to be very important that we are respectful of where children start from, join with them on their own terms, and try to understand the world from their point of view rather than filter it through our understanding. We aim to do this by:

- looking for opportunities to give children their own voice
- listening to that voice without being confused by the problem. The problems are the problems, not the people. We need to be especially careful not to let a problem story represent the totality of the person
- refusing to 'sum children up', remaining uncertain, open to contradictions, and to possibilities
- speaking with children as active agents in the creation of their lives, worlds and selves
- avoiding assumptions that might limit their potential, such as ideas about deficit, pathology or any single label.

Our basic values include a strong belief in kindness, dignity and a constant search for each child's uniqueness (see also Kelsey and McEwing 2008).

Chapter Three

Setting Achievable Goals

This chapter discusses the importance of constructing helpful and realistic goals and describes different ways of doing this. Developing well-formed goals for work with children is a vital aspect in increasing best outcomes, but it can also be one of the most difficult things to do. Children sometimes don't know what their best hopes are, or things may be so difficult in their lives that they can't imagine life being better, or they may be too ashamed or embarrassed to talk about their hopes and wishes. Equally, they can be overwhelmed by the expectations of those around them such as parents and professionals, or simply not see that there is a problem at all. We describe various techniques to help you develop goals in these difficult situations.

Agreeing goals

It is important to have clear goals, as otherwise you will have no way of knowing whether or not your work has been effective. A simple way of doing this is by asking:

- How will you know that meeting with me will be worthwhile?
- What will you notice?
- What are your best hopes?
- What will need to happen for you to know that our work is helpful to you?
- What will other people notice?

It is easier to measure whether or not you and a child have achieved your goals if you have defined them in clear, concrete behavioural changes, for example, 'I will be talking to my mum in a calm way; I will be behaving in a respectful way.' These broad goals are then developed by asking the child how they will be talking when they are calm: 'Suppose I looked through a window into your house and saw you being calm. What would I see, what would you be doing? What does being respectful look like?' This helps to ensure that there are no misunderstandings or misinterpretations by the worker of what calm and respectful behaviour means to the child. It also helps the child talk through what they will actually be doing when their best hopes are achieved, increasing the child's personal responsibility taking. This breakdown will make the goals appear small and achievable in contrast to one large over-arching goal, which at the beginning of the work can feel unreachable and overwhelming.

This doesn't mean that your goals will always be modest ones. It simply means that you and the child will start out with the simplest, most easily achievable goal. For example, one young person told Judith that his best hope was to meet the Dalai Lama. In answer to the question 'Suppose you have made a start towards this hope, what would I see that would be different, what would you be doing?' he thought for a while and then replied, 'I'd be going round the travel agents.' Having found out how much the trip would cost him, he then set himself another goal: to get out of bed and get a job and not waste his money on cannabis any more. This was not only an ethical, achievable, measurable and desirable goal, it was also one that kept his dreams and best hopes alive. These may change and develop, but without small goals that-make-a-start, those dreams can never be realized.

Both children and the adults in their lives have a tendency to describe goals negatively, such as, 'I won't be wetting the bed any more; Charlie will stop shouting at me.' Again, it is easier to measure whether or not you have been effective if your goals are framed in terms of the presence or start of something rather than absence or end of something. For example, it is more useful to talk about the start of dry beds than the end of wet beds (where it is impossible to say when it will happen). A more positive goal for dealing with Charlie's shouting could be developed by asking, 'What do you want Charlie to do instead of shouting?' And sometimes we simply ask, 'If this were a shop where you could buy a solution to your problem, what would you buy today?' It is possible to establish a goal even when a child cannot bring themselves to say what the problem is. For example, seven-year-old Maisie said it was a secret so rather than speculate about what the secret might possibly be, Judith simply asked, 'When everything is sorted and the secret isn't worrying you any more, what will be different?'

Sometimes workers, and their managers, confuse outputs (what services they are providing) with outcomes (what is different as a result of those services). This can lead to confusion; for example, a child goes to anger management classes but their behaviour does not change. However, the child has done what was asked of him and could well resent still being in trouble. So professionals working with children and their families need to be very clear about their goals, and able to provide a description of what 'preferred' behaviour will look like rather than just the absence of the 'problem' behaviour. We use the word 'instead' a great deal to help adults become clearer about their goals. For example: 'He won't be disrupting the class any more' will be developed by asking, 'When he's not disrupting the class any more, what will he be doing instead? And what else?' When goals are defined in this way, children often look relieved and say, 'I can do that.'

Families should also receive clear messages about exactly what needs to be different for the worker to be confident that their work is finished. This includes what small signs they will notice in parents' and children's behaviour to warrant a reduction in professional concerns. Again, it helps if this is phrased in positive rather than negative terms.

Practice activity

After a nine-month absence, Graeme has been permitted to have two hours supervised contact once a fortnight with his three-year-old son, Kyle, at a contact centre. Kyle runs to his father, who swings him in the air and gives him a big hug. Graeme takes Kyle into the hall where Kyle climbs into a toy car and Graeme pushes him round and round the hall. They both make a lot of noise and the supervisor is concerned that Kyle is getting over-excited.

How could the supervisor express this concern in positive, constructive terms?

It is equally important for the child/family to be given the opportunity to say how best professionals can support them and what needs to be different to increase the likelihood of the preferred outcome being achieved. Parents often ask that professionals turn up on time; that there will be no hidden agendas; and that a clear understanding be given of what needs to be different for the family if they are to no longer need professional intervention. We have found that this sharing of responsibility of what everyone involved could do to achieve the best outcome has encouraged a greater collaborative relationship with families. Allowing sufficient time to work out exactly what needs to happen for children to flourish is important in this process. Goals do change and develop further over time, but must always be achievable, time-limited, and measurable, otherwise you don't really know what you are doing.

More questions to aid goal setting

- What sort of person do you want to be?
- What can you see yourself doing when you will be doing [the goal], right here today?
- What will people notice that will be different when you are doing [goal]?
- How might they respond differently to you?
- How do you think this will be helpful to you?
- When will be the first opportunity to do [goal]?
- How will you know when you don't need to come here any more?
- How will I know that you don't need to come here any more?

The miracle question

De Shazer (1988, p.5) gave this name to a specific question that has been shown to work particularly well in developing goals. It is quite long and similar to a guided night-time fantasy, so is especially useful in helping children who struggle to say what their best hopes are. We don't use the word 'miracle' when asking this question because we often work with children who may well have been sexually abused and we are aware that associating words like 'miracle' or 'magic' with bedtime could be totally inappropriate in these instances. We use the words 'something wonderful' instead. Although it sounds formulaic, the miracle question works well because it is a curious question; you can never be sure what the answer will be. It goes like this:

> Now, I want to ask you a strange question. Suppose that while you are sleeping tonight and the entire house is quiet, a miracle happened. The miracle is that the problem which brought you here is solved. However, because you are sleeping, you don't know that the miracle has happened. So when you wake up tomorrow morning what will be different that will tell you that the miracle has happened and the problem which brought you here is solved?

This is a big question in that it is the start of a new story of how life is going to be for the child so it helps to ask it in the following way:

- Speak slowly and gently, in a soft voice, to give the child time to shift from a problem focus to a solution focus.

- Mark the beginning of a solution-building process clearly and dramatically by introducing the miracle question as unusual or strange.

- Use frequent pauses, allowing the child time to absorb the question and process his or her experiences through its different parts.

- Because the question asks for a description of the future, use future-directed words: What would be different? What will be signs of the miracle?

- When probing and asking follow-up questions, frequently repeat the phrase 'A miracle happens and the problem that brought you here is solved,' in order to reinforce the transition to solution talk.

- When children lapse into problem talk, gently refocus their attention on what will be different in their lives when the miracle happens.

(de Jong and Berg 2008, p.85)

Discussing what will be happening that is different may be the child's first opportunity to actually consider what life could be like, and rehearse this; for example, when a child responds with 'I'll be happy', you will follow up with questions about 'doing happiness': 'What are you doing when you are happy? How do other people know that you are happy?' Similarly, when a parent says, 'I will be having fun with my children,' follow-up questions would include: 'When you are having fun, what sort of things will you be doing? How will you plan for these fun times'? Therefore, a helpful goal will refer to some other behaviour that the person is hoping to see or do.

As children's perceptions of themselves are highly influenced by those around them, goal-setting questions can include other people in the child's life. A question can be asked such as, 'What would your mum notice differently about you?' For younger children, pets or favourite toys can also be used, for example, 'What would teddy see you doing when you are behaving in an OK way?' An answer may be very simple, but still constitute a desirable and measurable goal, for example, 'I will be sitting at my desk listening to my teacher' or 'I will be eating my dinner at the table.' Sometimes answers to the miracle question provide dramatic and immediate solutions, like when ten-year-old Ian said he would be coming downstairs with a smile on his face and his brother would not be teasing him at breakfast. His mother immediately commented that if he came downstairs with a smile on his face, she would stop his brother teasing him. Despite Ian having long-standing, serious behaviour problems, he and his mum worked out both their goal and solution (better behaviour) from this one small conversation (for a fuller account, see Milner 2001, p.14). Equally children often struggle to think what would be different so we list below some follow-up questions.

Miracle question prompts:

- What will you notice; what else; what else; what else?
- What will you see?
- What will be different?
- What will other people notice about you?
- Picture later in the morning: what is happening now; what else is telling you the miracle has happened?
- At school/home/other places, what is different here?
- Back at home, late afternoon, what do you notice now?
- What sort of things are you saying to yourself at the end of the day?

For unrealistic answers like 'winning the lottery', 'all the teachers will have been sacked', 'I'll have absolute power':

- So, what will *you* be doing differently then?
- Can any of this happen now?

Variations on the miracle question

There are several variants of the miracle question, but shortened or crystal ball versions do not seem to work as well, probably because they don't encourage enough detail of what will be different. This detail is important in helping children discover solutions and ideas they did not know they had and helps them talk themselves into change. One version of the miracle question that we find especially helpful with children is a *Back to the Future* question. This was inspired by the time machine in the Michael J. Fox film of the same name and changes regularly to keep up to date with popular science fiction films and television programmes. Essentially, it is a way by which children can consult their older, wiser selves and it goes like this:

> *Suppose today I'm still busy with some other kid but don't like to keep you sitting around so I offer you a ride in the Tardis. You set off with the Doctor and when the doors open, you are right outside your house. You creep up to the window and look inside. Imagine your shock when you see yourself, two years older [choose an age that is appropriate for the solution and child's capacity to think ahead]. You can tell that this person has life totally sorted out. She/he looks so happy. What is she/he doing that tells you this?*

In the ensuing discussion, get as much detail as possible by asking what they are doing, who is with them, what the room looks like, whose photographs are on the wall, etc. and then you have their goal. To obtain their solution, ask 'You know how it is when someone is watching you? They get a sense of it so you turn round and they see you peering through the window' [don't worry about both the 'yous', the child will know which one you are talking about]. The child says to you, 'Oh, wow, it's me when I was in all that trouble/was so sad/felt such a failure/etc. Come in, come in.' You say, 'I haven't got long because I'm seeing this person about it all in a minute. But I must know, how *did* you do it?'

Most children can answer this question immediately because they have now been talking about their older, competent self at some length. For those children who struggle to answer the question, they can be invited to ask their older, wiser self for advice on comfort: 'Okay, so you can't tell me yet, but can you tell me how you got through this difficult time?' This invites the child to work out what would be comforting during the current difficulties. Additionally, because you added the word 'yet' in this question, you are presupposing that the child will be able to answer the question at some time in the future.

Prompts for 'don't know' answers to 'how did you do it?'

- Look puzzled and wait.
- It's a difficult question…
- Maybe you know and don't know at the same time, that's hard to say…
- Take your time and think about it, there's no rush.
- Guess.
- Suppose you did know, what would the answer be?

- Perhaps I've not asked this question in a helpful way, how could I ask it better?
- What advice would you give to a person with a similar problem to you?
- Perhaps you might like to study what happens next time and see if you can spot how you did it.
- Okay, so what would [name of loved one] say about it?

Group miracle questions

The miracle question can also be used with groups of young people. Sharry (2001, p.136) suggests asking group members to close their eyes, relax each muscle in turn, and visualize a relaxing scene before asking the miracle question. Then they are asked to imagine the new solution situation in detail:

> *You are going to be surprised at all the differences and changes you notice... So what do you notice first?... What tells you the miracle has happened?... How do you feel different?... What do you notice is different about other people? ...and so on.*

After the visualization process, members discuss the differences in pairs, and then in the whole group. The advantage of this is that the solutions generated by group members are likely to have common links and this can be reinforcing when shared in the whole group. Also hearing other people's miracles can be motivating and inspiring and encourage young people to develop their own. Don't worry if the group format encourages silliness; it will start the group thinking and they may need time to work out their goals – as is seen in the case example below:

Case example ————————————————

Judith was working with a group of young women excluded from mainstream education, misusing substances, and at risk of being drawn into prostitution. They had no idea what their goals for the group might be, so Judith asked the most vocal young woman the miracle question. Marie's miracle day turned out to be one where she would be 16 and not have to attend school, not living at home, and having an endless supply of drugs and drink without having to pay for them. Rather than tell Marie that this was an unacceptable goal, Judith puzzled with Marie about how her goal would fit with her teachers' worries about the group: concerns about safety. This enabled all the young women to talk about how they did or didn't manage to keep themselves safe when they were misusing substances, and they developed a group goal around increasing safety.

Although the miracle question had yielded only one goal that was immediately useable, the young women insisted that any new group member 'do the miracle thing' and their 'keeping safe' goal broadened their individual goals, these being increasingly talked about as 'getting a life', reducing arguments with parents, handling boyfriends, and 'getting some work done so I can pass my exams'. (Milner 2004, p.15)

Agreeing goals with children who don't want to talk to you

Formulating goals is not always straightforward and can be a tricky task. A good way to start goal-setting with children is to look at the things that they are already doing well and frame a goal of keeping these things going and building on this to include those new behaviours. If you start from a stance that someone is already achieving some things, this generates optimism and confidence that can be built upon. This is especially important when you are working out goals with children who don't want to talk to you for one reason or another.

Where children do not consider that they have a problem, it is still important to listen to what is significant to them. Children usually have good reasons for not wanting to talk to you: embarrassment, fear of consequences, possibility of losing face, shame, etc. but providing a space for the young person makes them feel respected so they may become more motivated to engage in the work (Saleeby 2007). This space allows you to discover the child's own way of cooperating with you. And we have discovered lots of different forms of cooperation. For example, Natalie preferred to sit on the stairs and 'overhear' while Judith asked her foster carer what she thought would be different when Natalie was not causing her a great deal of concern. Although Jamie and Boris could bear to stay in the sitting room, they made some distance for themselves. Boris stood in the doorway and talked to Judith, who was sitting on a sofa to his left, in the mirror opposite them both. Jamie stood by the window with his back to her. They had different reasons for this, but it didn't matter; this was how they talked to people about their problems at that point in their lives.

Whilst it is always preferable to keep your work as simple, brief and least intrusive as possible, sometimes more creativity is needed in helping children set goals. Below we describe some of the techniques we have devised or borrowed. Before reading these, test out your own creativity and other skills you have developed in working with children so that these can to be used to devise your own techniques for effective goal setting.

Practice activity

- Make a list of all your best skills (be specific but not modest).
- How do these help you to be helpful to the children you work with?
- Choose one of these skills.
- How can you enhance this skill to make it a bit more effective?
- What would you have to do?
- When can you do it by?
- How would the children you are working with know that you are doing it better?

(Myers 2008, p.9)

Children who can see no future for themselves

A child who is struggling with depression and/or trauma may be so overwhelmed with how things are right now that they find it difficult to think what life could be like. As an alternative, enquiries can be made into how the child is coping, how they are managing to get up in the morning when they are experiencing so much pain and anguish. Whilst it would insensitive, and ineffective, to press a child for a goal in these circumstances, it is possible to hint that the future may be easier by adding a little hopefulness to coping questions, such as:

- That must be scary/terrible/worrying [then add] *at the moment* or *at this time*.
- Have you ever felt like this before? How did you get over it *last time*?

- So, you've not been able to beat…*so far*?
- How have stopped things getting worse?
- How are you managing to carry on *despite* …?
- But you still managed to get to school; how did you find this determination?

Working with children who have self-harmed in some way, or are talking about ending it all, can be scary for the worker. In telling you about their intent, the child is handing you the responsibility for their life continuing. This is an enormous responsibility so, even where you suspect that the child is not really serious – young people, particularly, have a tendency to catastrophize – there is a temptation to hand over the problem to a specialist mental health service. Before you do this, you may like to consider using a graded set of questions devised by John Hendon (2005) for assessing levels of risk in these situations, and follow-up questions to help the child or young person begin to move away from suicidal thoughts.

RISK ASSESSMENT QUESTIONS FOR CHILDREN WITH SUICIDAL THOUGHTS

- At this point, how much more do you feel you can cope with?
- How far is this getting you down right now?
- How often, recently, have you felt you are getting to the end of your tether?
- At the moment, how far do you feel able to go on?
- How close do you feel, right now, to ending your life?

For older children:

- If you decided to go ahead with the last resort option, what method would you use? How prepared are you should you decide? (Paradoxically, having made preparations is indicative of both very high risk and low risk as some people are comforted by being prepared and therefore do not feel the need to go ahead with the last resort option.)

FOLLOW-UP QUESTIONS ONCE SUICIDAL INTENT HAS BEEN ESTABLISHED

- Tell me about a time in the last week when you felt least suicidal?
- Before you were feeling as you do at the moment, what did you do in the day that interested you?

- What has stopped you taking your life up to this point?
- On a scale of 1–10 (1=most suicidal and 10=least suicidal), how suicidal do you feel right now?
- On a scale of 1–10, how suicidal were you before you decided to seek help?
- What would you be doing/thinking/feeling to be another half point higher?
- What have you done in the last week that has made a difference to the terrible situation you are in?
- On a scale of 1–10 (1=can't be bothered and 10=will do anything it takes), how determined are you to give another option a try first?
- Let us suppose you went for the last resort option and actually died. You are at your own funeral as a spirit looking down from about 10 feet at the mourners below. What might you be thinking about another option you could have tried first? At this funeral, who would be the most upset among the mourners? What advice would they have wanted to give you regarding other options?
- When was the last time, before this time, that you thought of ending it all?
- What did you do that made a difference and enabled you to pull yourself back?
- Suicide is the last resort as we know, what other ways have you tried so far to crack this problem?

It can be difficult to set goals in other forms of self-harm, such as eating difficulties or cutting, because these behaviours also confer some status on the young person amongst their friends. Or sometimes, a whole group of friends will decide to start cutting. Anything to do with body image is always going to be affected by media images, especially being thin, but it is worth remembering that people do like to decorate their skin. Children have always enjoyed putting transfers on their arms and now aspire to proper tattoos like their football and pop star heroes. This means that a child can be feeling both hopeless *and* competent when they are making cuts on their arm. Martin Selekman (2002) recommends asking the young person to invite a famous guest of their choice to act as their consultant. Having chosen their guest consultant, the young person is then asked what advice that person would give them. Obviously the famous guest cannot advise the young person to do more harmful things, so this is one way of reducing the impact of media messages. Frederike Jacob (2001) asks people with eating disorders, 'Tell me what is useful about it?', 'What does it enable you to do differently?'

Acknowledging that some problems have advantages as well as disadvantages is useful where children are extremely pessimistic, especially when followed up with, 'How can you keep the advantages but get rid of the disadvantages?' Where the young person is unable to respond to any of the questions above, we have found that asking them to 'take a small step in a direction that will be good for them' and come back and tell us when they have done this, is helpful in removing the misery block which is preventing the young person working out a goal for themselves. Some young people seem so immersed in the details of their misery that they can talk about little else. This becomes isolating because the friends who initially offered support become bored with the same problem description and irritated at their advice not being taken. In these situations, we acknowledge the extent of their difficulties and then make it clear that we will talk about different things from now on:

- [looking back at our notes] Yes, I've got that. You told me that already.

- [the misery tale continues] Yes, I've got that. You told me that already.

- [the misery tale continues] We have spent a lot of time looking at the awful situation you are in. I'm wondering how useful this is? I'm thinking that it's a bit like trying to clear out a cupboard and then putting everything back, instead of sorting what needs to stay, what needs mending and what needs throwing away. So, I wondered if you'd mind if we shut the door of the misery cupboard for a while and looked in the happiness cupboard instead? What might we find in that cupboard?

- [if more than one thing is suggested] Tell me more about that happiness, how can you start get more of it?

- [if the cupboard is pretty empty] It looks like we'll have to go shopping for some happiness. What would you like to buy first?

Children with unachievable hopes

We have previously mentioned the importance of goals being achievable. However, children (and parents) can choose a preferred future that is both out of their control and therefore unachievable. Such an example may be a child opting for a goal of his mum and dad getting back together. Instead of negotiating the goal, an alternative form of enquiry could be, 'I can understand that you want your mum and dad back together, but if this was something that didn't happen how do you think you would manage/cope? What is your fall back plan? What could your mum and dad do that would make the changes easier for you?'

Similar coping questions are also helpful to explore when someone has been bereaved and states that their goal would be for this person to be alive again, 'Supposing [name of the person who has died] is looking down from heaven right now. She/he's going to be pretty worried about you. What advice would they give you for handling this problem right now?'

Prompts for children living with difficulties that have to be coped with

- Each day I'd like you to do one small thing that is good for you. We'll talk about what difference it makes.

- Each day notice what else you do that is good for you, so we can talk about it.

- Could you keep track of the good choices you make so we can talk about them?

- As you are not yet able to defeat the problem, what can you do to stop it growing, or to make it wait (so you will be taking a little control back for yourself)? What would be the smallest step you could take?

- Perhaps you could pretend you have a future and notice the difference, so we can talk about it. What you will be doing instead of what you do now?

- What can you do that will be kind to yourself and hard on the problem? What will you be doing, or feeling, differently?

- Problems try to control us, so maybe you could confuse the problem by taking some control of your own thoughts? Think up some things to say to yourself that will help you to stand up to the problem and its lies. I'll be interested in what you come up with.

Where a child is receiving palliative care for a terminal illness, the quality of the remaining time is vital, so establishing the child's goals is a matter of urgency. Gardiner (1977) outlines the rights of a dying child:

- To know the truth about the probable outcome of their illness or, as most children have already worked it out for themselves, to affirm the truth.
- To share thoughts about dying – not just the probability of death but the many questions that follow.
- To live as full and normal a life as possible.
- To participate in the process of dying. To have a say whether treatment continues or not and in whether to die in hospital, at home or in a hospice.

The goals of the dying child will change as they do in other circumstances, so some questions could include:

- What ideas do you have about what comes after this life?
- How will things look better for you when you have worked out what it will look like?
- How do you want your life to be between now and [next week, next month, etc.]?
- What are your best achievements?
- What hopes do you still have?
- What do you best want to be remembered for?
- What small changes in living will make a big difference for you?

Where there are conflicting goals

When working with groups or families there is a possibility that there will be varied and, at times, conflicting hopes for the work. Instead of attempting to formulate this into one over-arching group goal, it is helpful to explore individual hopes and wishes and then prioritize these as you would when working with one person who has several goals. Again it is important to ensure that the framing of questions is done within the context of the future and, therefore, indicating that something different can happen. You can brainstorm this with a flipchart (it helps if a parent or an older child gets to write things down) or you may prefer to use the technique described below.

TALKING TO MABEL

This technique is named after a very wise dog Judith met. The family all had different ideas on what the problem was and what should be done about it, so Judith consulted with Mabel:

> *I've noticed that Mabel always sits in the middle of the room when we're talking quietly but when someone gets upset, she goes and sits near to them. She's obviously a very sensitive and caring dog. I wonder what she would say would be happening differently if she knew for certain that you were all alright and she could curl up and go to sleep in the middle of the room without having to worry about any of you?*

Shortened circular miracle question

This is particularly useful with families when you suspect that some family members are afraid/reluctant to voice their opinions, or where you are unsure that the children's opinions are their own or unduly influenced by their parents' views.

Before we ask the miracle question, we give everyone a piece of paper and a pencil and ask them to write down the answer to the question we are about to ask. Preschool children are invited to draw their answer; very young children are given a sheet of paper, stickers and crayons to make a picture which they can then present to an adult; and older children without speech are linked with another family member who the family has identified as the person best able to represent them. We keep this light-hearted by reminding them that no-one must see their answer and to put their arm round the paper as they would do at school to prevent copying. Then we ask: Suppose, while you are asleep tonight, a wonderful thing happens and everything that is worrying you [or your teachers, or social care, etc.] has disappeared. But because you were all fast asleep, you didn't notice this happening. What is the first thing that you would notice that would tell you that things are better?

Reminding everyone to keep their answers hidden, we then ask them in turn to guess what another person has written. This is not done randomly; we ask the most supportive parent to guess what the youngest child has said as this is relatively non-threatening and gives that parent the opportunity to demonstrate his/her understanding of the child's needs and wishes. Then we ask the most confident child to guess what the most powerful family member may have put. Finally we ask this family member what they think another child has said (we usually select the most vulnerable child here). Where families give superficial answers, such as 'He would have a new bike,' we consult the family pet, even if it has to be an imaginary one. After this has been talked about, we ask each person what they actually put and discuss differences of perceptions. This exercise has several advantages:

- It gives children the opportunity to express their needs and wishes.
- It enables parents to hear these.
- It encourages discussion about what changes can be made.
- It enables a parent to discuss differences of opinion without fear of being contradicted or put down.
- It provides a snapshot of family dynamics in action.

The latter observations are important as they reveal family strengths (e.g., a parent being unexpectedly caring towards a child) and areas for improvement (e.g., the children fighting and the parents unable to handle this). It is less threatening to suggest an area for improvement as a possible goal during the exercise, and parents enjoy their competencies being noticed and commented upon. Numerous hopes usually emerge so it is important to highlight what would be the first sign of the goals happening, and prioritize all the goals. This will ensure no-one becomes overwhelmed or confused with what they are working towards.

Children with learning difficulties

When we are starting work with a child with learning difficulties, adults often tell us that the child doesn't concentrate well. We find that such children can concentrate for 30 to 40 minutes as long as we remember to go at a suitable pace, use appropriate materials and make it fun. People with learning difficulties do not function at all well when they are stressed, so we allow children ten minutes of settling down time.

Depending on the form the anxiety takes this could consist of allowing silly behaviour, simply getting out our materials and talking about them in a neutral sort of way, or asking the child to undertake a simple task, such as taking care of our coat.

The basic principle is to reduce the speed of everything by:

- talking more slowly and repeating or rephrasing important points several times
- using pictures or symbols to explain complex concepts such as thoughts and emotions
- explaining ourselves through written or drawn materials as many children find this method of communicating less threatening than face-to-face conversations
- taking time to learn new behaviours so that short chunks of information are repeated several times and in fresh ways. Charts and stickers act as useful visual reminders
- helping the child understand new situations by keeping changes to the minimum
- providing opportunities to practise newly learned behaviours.

Cartooning makes it easier for a child with learning difficulties to develop a clear vision and sense of control over future events. Here a large sheet of paper is divided into six squares and the child is invited to draw the problem in the first square, how they would rather be in the second, a 'mighty helper' in the third, what a slip back might look like in the fourth, how it is handled in the fifth, and how success will be celebrated in the sixth (Berg and Steiner 2003). We also use I Can Do cards (www.innovativeresources.org), which are a younger version of the Strengths cards discussed in Chapter 2; Mr Men; right road/wrong road pictures; and joint story writing.

Sometimes we use several techniques over a few discussions with the child before a clear goal is agreed.

Case example

Fourteen-year-old Ricky was small for his age and walked with some difficulty because of cerebral palsy. He had a statement of educational need, but it wasn't exactly clear how limited his intellectual functioning was as he had never cooperated long enough to complete psychological tests.

His life with an abusive birth family had been very traumatic, with many changes of school, and he had experienced several foster care breakdowns since coming into care so his intellectual functioning could also have been affected by his life experiences, and was not necessarily fixed at a low level. Now with very experienced foster carers, he was testing them to the limit by swearing at them in the home, and making sexually inappropriate comments to complete strangers when outside. He was also excluded from his special school for similar behaviours.

Ricky didn't particularly like face-to-face communication, responding to questions with phrases he had picked up from television, such as 'choose life', so Judith asked him to help her make a six-square cartoon of his problems. In square one, he drew a rudimentary picture of himself with lots of hair. He told her that he doesn't have a problem but 'these two do' (indicating his foster carers). Judith asked him to draw what the problem which is bothering his foster carers looks like, starting him off with a speech bubble for 'sexy comments' and a few swear words floating around in the picture he drew. Prompted by his carers, he added further inappropriate words he uses (slag, suck). He then drew a picture of himself without the problem, needing much prompting to write down the words he would be using instead of sexually inappropriate comments and swearing. Slowly he added thank you, hello, goodbye, please, excuse me. He found it very hard to think of who he needed to help him, but eventually drew what looked like a little angel. Ricky insisted it was a ghost called Bin Laden. He became stuck when attempting to draw the ghost helping him, so Judith helped him consolidate what he had already done. She made a list of the 'acceptable' words he identified and provided the foster carers with a book of stickers to add to the list to mark any successes, plus a small bag of sweets to reward any reduction in swearing/increase in use of acceptable words.

At the next session, Ricky's swearing was at the same level, but he had managed some polite words – three pleases, four thank yous, two no thank yous and one yes gaff. He readily agreed that he could do more of it as he had been delighted to find out that a 'Please may I have a bacon sandwich?' worked better than 'Get me a bacon sandwich.' He was still answering questions with set phrases, so Judith asked Ricky what he would be doing when he has 'chosen a life' and, with his foster carers' assistance, he was able to list several goals for a good life:

- being in the right school
- living with his foster carers
- keeping his sense of humour
- being polite and helpful
- laughing
- having a girlfriend
- being a bit calmer
- being gentle
- having a bit of supervision
- breaking up motor cars
- having a career as a mechanic.

He was also able to list what he wanted to get rid of:

- silliness
- swearing
- the inappropriate problem (his description of his sexual comments to strangers)
- anger
- laziness.

Ricky chose 'being more gentle' as his starting point for his new life. He thought that the ghost in his cartoon could help by living in the first drawer of his bed to take up his nasty thoughts so he could come downstairs in a good mood. He thought he would be smiling and saying, 'Good morning, could I have a bacon sandwich?'

Children with complex physical needs

However disabled a child is they can, and should, be helped to take responsibility for their own health and make informed choices and decisions about their health and well-being (DoH and DFES 2004). The National Service Framework also wants to see professionals listening carefully and attempting to see the world from their perspective (Bates 2005). Effective communication with children about their health care needs not only dispels misconceptions and anxieties, but, says Matthews (2006), ultimately improves their health care experience. There is a big responsibility for the nursing practitioner here because doctors tend to talk to parents rather than children about their medical conditions (Elliot and Watson 2000), and while some general practitioners attempt to consider a child's understanding, and engage the child in discussion, this is an exception rather than the rule (Tates, Meeuwesen and Bensing 2002).

Facilitating the child's participation is by no means straightforward, especially when they are young. For example, young children often use play as a diversion from pain and coping mechanism so pain needs to be assessed before attempts are made to establish goals through play. On the other hand, blind children are often still and quiet as they attempt to make sense of new situations, therefore 'quietness' probably means that they are concentrating (Orr 2003). Even where a child's needs are complex, this does not mean that the child cannot be fully involved in setting goals for their care and well-being. For example, Katherine is 16 years old and has tubersclerosis with associated epilepsy and learning disabilities. Having been on the receiving end of many assessments, her mother comments:

> In an ideal world, I would like to meet the person and I would like the person to meet Katherine and get to know her. Play games and do things that Katherine enjoys doing before she actually did the assessment so Katherine would have a bond with her. (Roulstone 2001, p.15)

The Mencap report *Death by Indifference* (2007) found that hospital care for patients like Katherine can be poor, but communication and continuity of care can be much improved when a traffic lights system is used. This is a simple colourful form which identifies important 'must know' information, including how to communicate with the person, their mental capacity, how to recognize pain and offer comfort, and their likes and dislikes (for more information see Michael (2008); DoH (2009); or contact Ruth Bell, Specialist Practitioner Community Learning Disability Nurse, Oldham Community Health Services).

Practice activity

Think of a disabled child you are working with. What games does the child like to play? How could you use those games to involve the child more fully in making decisions about their health and well-being?

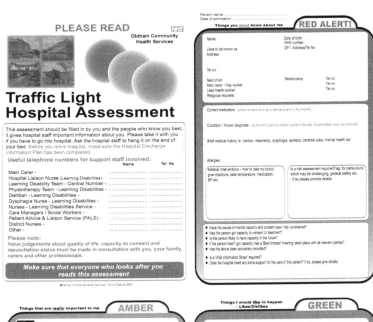

Noisy groups and families

Customer Complaints Desk

This was invented by 12-year-old Ramone, the second oldest in a family of seven children, all of whom talked loudly and frequently at the same time so hardly anyone was ever listened to unless they threw a major tantrum. We were in the middle of a loud and disputed discussion on who had been most successful at responsibility taking during the previous week when Ramone nipped his nose between two fingers and said in a high, nasal tone: 'Will Ramone please report to the Customer Complaints Desk.' He then walked to the corner of the room and delivered his 'message' as an official announcement. Although the family members were not good at listening to each other, they were accustomed to listening to formal announcements so they all stopped talking and listened to Ramone. After this, other children would make customer announcements or we would call a child to the 'Customer Complaints Desk' when they particularly wanted to be heard.

Key points

- A significant principle of solution focused practice is that the goal(s) of the work is decided by the child. It is the skill of the worker to support the child in constructing their goals in such a way that there is a clear description of what will be different when their problems are eradicated or of less significance in their lives.

- It is important that goals are established as early as possible so that both the child and the worker have a collaborative understanding of the direction of the work. It is of equal importance that the goals are realistic and measurable. Unrealistic goals can create a situation of failure and if they are not measurable, how will you know when your support is no longer required? It is also helpful to begin this process by noticing those things that are already going well and developing and building on this with the inclusion of the desired new behaviours.

- A basic way to develop goals is to use the miracle question. This presents a future-orientated context, which invites the person to imagine what life could look like without the problem and thus identify their hopes for the work. The miracle question can also be applied within a group situation. However, any future-oriented questions will assist in the formation of sound goals.

- Sometimes young people can struggle to describe what would be different from their perspective, but asking them from the perspective of a third party, 'What would be the first thing your mum would notice that would be different?' can often spur them on.

- A final issue to take into consideration is the possibility of goals changing during the course of the work. This may be due to the young person gaining a clearer understanding of what would be most helpful for them to explore or that an initial goal has been achieved and within this process there is a realization that it would be beneficial for a further issue to be discussed to enable them to move forward.

Chapter Four

Finding Exceptions to Problems

This chapter introduces the practice principle of finding exceptions to difficulties. Locating, and recognizing, times when children have managed their behaviour in a way that is helpful and beneficial to them and others, are empowering and uplifting experiences which help engage children. There is further discussion on the importance of language: how we talk about problems; the recognition of strengths; and helping children begin to see themselves as separate from their difficulties. Techniques that support this process are also described.

Finding exceptions

Most problems have exceptions, so once goals are agreed the next step is to direct the conversation around exploring those times when the child's goals have happened and/or the problems they have experienced have not happened, or happened less. Focusing on those times, *the exceptions*, provides the child with an opportunity to realize that there have been better times, and that they have the required skills and strengths to tackle their problems. Furthermore, it reinforces the assumption, mentioned in earlier chapters, that children are experts in their own lives who are equipped with the knowledge necessary for finding ways of moving forward. Because they are accustomed to being told what to do about their problems (not that they necessarily do this), they are unused to being asked about their own solutions so they can struggle to locate this information. This is where the support and skill of the worker is required.

Solution focused practice recognizes that there are times when the problem, however entrenched, could have happened but didn't; identifying those times will therefore also identify each child's unique solution. If you think about something you have tried to give up, smoking or chocolate, for example, there will have been times when you could have had a cigarette or a second chocolate but you didn't. What probably happened is that neither you nor anyone else noticed this happening; or, if you did, you dismissed it as not good enough. This is because we get into the bad habit of noticing problems and ignoring solutions, causing problems to get bigger and bigger so that any tiny improvements seem irrelevant. This is very discouraging for people with problems. A solution focused conversation aims to discover even the smallest exception to the problem. Then the unique details of it are identified, such as what the child was thinking or doing that was different on those occasions. The purpose of this is to make those different circumstances much more visible and therefore memorable and accessible to use on the next occasion, with the aim of supporting the child in increasing the control they have over their problem and their life generally. The skill of the worker is in noticing the tiny beginnings of solutions and helping children 'literally talk themselves out of their troubles by encouraging them to describe their lives in new ways' (Miller 1997, p.6).

Case example

Kirsty complains that her six-year-old, Jadon, simply will not do what he is told. She describes a constant low level disobedience, which occasionally escalates into them shouting at each other. Then Jadon makes cruel remarks about her, at which point she becomes so upset that she sends him to his bedroom until he has calmed down and can apologize for his behaviour. This strategy doesn't work very well because he informs her that he 'isn't bothered' and although she doesn't send him to his room for longer than it takes for him to calm down, he often opts to stay in his bedroom rather than come downstairs and apologize. (Levy and O'Hanlon (2001), comment that defiant children can soak up much more negativity than their parents without getting anywhere near as upset.) Kirsty feels like a complete failure especially as – after a rocky start – Jadon is behaving well at school.

Judith: Your mum tells me that you got into trouble at school when you first went there but now your behaviour is really good. This is most interesting. Can you tell me how that happened?

Jadon: I was shouting in class. Matthew was shouting at me. He was swearing. Mrs Boden told us to stop and Matthew didn't, so I didn't. It's not fair. Matthew's always getting me into trouble.

Judith: [ignoring the conversational diversion about fairness] So how come your behaviour improved when you didn't take any notice of what Mrs Boden said?

Jadon: She sent me to the headteacher and then my behaviour got good.

Judith: How did you do that, turn it round like that?

Jadon: She told me to stop messing about in class and behave myself.

Judith: And you did?

Jadon: Yes.

Judith: Straight away?

Jadon: Yes.

Judith: Gosh, just like that? [Jadon nods] How did you do it?

Jadon: I just did it.

Judith: So how do you do behaving?

Jadon: Just behave.

Judith: Suppose I was looking through your classroom window, what would I see you doing that would tell me you were behaving?

Jadon: I wouldn't be shouting. Not messing about.

Judith: What do you do instead of shouting?

Jadon: Talk quietly.

Judith: What do you do instead of messing about?

Jadon: I ignore Matthew when he tries to get me into trouble. He's been to the headteacher *three* times!

Judith: How do you do ignoring Matthew?

Jadon: I just get on with my work.

Judith: And what else do you do for behaving?

Jadon: I do what Mrs Boden says.

Judith: First time of asking?

Jadon: Yes. And I listen.

Judith: So you can do six-year-old behaving at school. It might even be seven-year-old behaving! What else do well-behaved six-year-olds do?

After getting a lot more detail from Jadon about how he does behaving at school, what the consequences of this are for him, and whether it suits him to be like this, Judith then begins to look at other aspects of six-year-old behaving, such as at the supermarket, friends' homes, and then his own home. Although, of course, if he chooses to do five-year-old behaving first or only do as mum says at the second or third time of asking, that's okay because he's beginning to change. We are quite happy to start off slowly with small steps. The solution focused process is a bit like making a snowman: if you pay enough attention to packing the snow into a tight ball to begin with, it quickly picks up more and more snow. Jadon's small beginning will soon gather pace.

Changing problem stories into solution stories

Talking is a powerful instrument. When we describe something in negative terms then we construct a negative image of the child as well as the problem. Even designating a stair step as the naughty step is a negative way of helping a child to calm down; why not call it the calming step, or the well-behaved step? There is the danger here of children, and the adults in their lives, beginning to think of themselves as bad children, or sick children, or children somehow lacking. Talking this way can also separate parents and children. Where someone has to be blamed, then parents generally prefer to have the child labelled as the problem rather than themselves as possible failures as parents. These images and labels can limit children's potential for growth; for example, we hear children telling us that they can't concentrate because they have ADHD at the same time as they are concentrating like mad as they talk with us. However, if we talk with children about how they have coped with a situation, or successfully negotiated a difficulty, and identify with them the resources that they have drawn upon, then the conversation shifts into one of optimism and achievement.

It is vital that the details of any exception are explored vigorously by asking what, when, where, how, when and who questions. Exploring for exceptions brings people's competencies to their attention that may otherwise remain lost or hidden. We often hear from parents that their children are displaying disruptive behaviour at school but that this is not experienced within the home environment and visa versa. Within this context questions related to what's different are relevant, focusing on what has been going well and how they did this so that they can do more of it. It also highlights to children that there have been successes (successes related to their hopes and best wishes and what's going well for them and not successes which have been constructed and decided by the adults around them) and this is noticed. *Noticing* progress and/or success is a very important skill in solution focused practice. What has been noticed is discussed in a spirit of genuine curiosity: 'Tell me more about this,' 'How did you do it?,' 'Did anyone else notice this?,' 'Was it hard or easy to do?' We do not praise the child at this point or offer any suggestions as to how the child could do more of the exception. Instead we would say something like, 'I'm impressed, are you?' The child may be not at all impressed and want more for themselves, so goals may need to be revisited. Where the child is pleased with the exception, we would say something like: 'Did you know this about yourself?', 'What does doing this tell you about you as a person?' This sort of conversation encourages the child to take responsibility for their own behaviour and to learn more about their personal qualities, skills and abilities.

Case example

Sophia has always suffered from eczema which has been controlled by conventional medicines. Now 13, she is unable to sleep because of the itch, is too tired to go school, and is scratching herself severely. Her medication cannot be increased as it is reaching toxic levels so she has been referred to a counsellor, David Epston. He notices an exception early on in his interview with her, because although she says she has a fair bit of itchiness on both arms, she is not scratching. David observes that as she is not sitting on her hands, she must be using her mind to stop herself from itching. He does not compliment her on this achievement; instead he asks more curious questions:

- Am I right in thinking you have a good mind?
- What's good about your mind? (She answers that she's determined.)
- I expect you will need a lot of determination to fight a problem that weakens a young person's hopes – you think you've won and it still comes back?
- Say you went free of it for a while, would you be able to predict when it would get particularly bad again? (For a fuller account, see Freeman *et al.* 1997, pp.166–267.)

Such conversations increase the likelihood of hope and engagement and thus have potential for change. For example, when there are concerns about a parent's ability to keep a child safe it is much more productive to support changes and move things forward when the worker focuses on those times when levels of safety have increased. In contrast, if the conversations consistently centre on the presence of unsafe behaviour it is likely to promote 'problem talk' as well as make the parent feel like a failure which could then move them into a position of thinking, 'What's the point?' This is not to say that we should ignore unsafe behaviour as ultimately a child's safety is of paramount importance; however, if the plan is for the child to remain at home with the requirement that specific changes are required, the focus of conversation remains on questions such as, 'When things are going wrong, what do you do to move them forward?' For example, if you were struggling with managing your time and the focus of the conversations with your manager was centred on your failure to get a report done on time or meet other deadlines, how would that make you feel? And how helpful would that be in supporting you in meeting deadlines in the future? Conversely, if the conversation focused on times when you have met, or come close to meeting deadlines, helping you discover what was different on those occasions, you are likely to feel more confident that you can do this again. Such a conversation would also help to bring your attention to a detailed plan of action that works best for you. Furthermore, discussions centred on what is/was different begin to construct a description of what life could be like and the differing experiences and possibilities.

Where a child can identify a deliberate exception and pinpoint specifically what and how they did it, the next question is obvious, 'Can you do more of it?' However, lots of children have difficulty with answering 'how they did it' questions, saying things like, 'Well, I just did it,' or 'It just happened'; so more questions are needed.

Prompt questions for when children are stuck

- Tell me about the times you are *not* …
- Tell me about the times you are *less* …
- Tell me about the times you can cope *despite* this feeling …
- When you feel like…and you don't, what do you do?
- How did you do that?
- Tell me about a time you refuse to let [the problem] ruin your day.
- When was the last time you that you stopped [the problem] from spoiling your day?
- What will it be like when [the exception] is happening more?
- Who will notice when [the exception] is happening more?
- Who could help you do [the exception] more?

Some children persist in denying the existence of any exceptions, especially where they have got into the habit of acting tough about their problem. This can be countered by expressing your amazement that they can maintain this state: 'What, you never get your homework in on time? Never? It must take a lot of organizational skill to make sure that you don't slip up. Sounds to me like a lot of hard work.' Then you can have a conversation about the child's ability to plan and work hard before moving the conversation lightly on to a more constructive tack with something like: 'Have you ever thought of having a short break from all this effort you are making every day?' As we mentioned earlier, humour is a useful tool, especially when a child doesn't want to back down from an entrenched position and lose face. There are a few situations where the child genuinely cannot find an exception, for example, where a child has an extreme fear of needles. In these instances, success in a situation requiring the same resources can be explored, so we would ask questions such as, 'What is the bravest thing you have ever done?' Bravery is a transferable resource for tackling many problems. It is also useful to make enquiries of other people who are present in their lives as the following example shows.

Case example ────────────────────────────────

Fifteen-year-old Paul requested support in managing his frustrations better as they were spoiling his relationships with his girlfriend and his mum. He had a specific goal: he wanted to manage stressful and difficult situations better. He lacked detail of what this would look like, so the initial conversation helped him define and frame his goals around what he would be doing more of (instead of less of), when the problem was less, what he would be doing differently. Paul said that he would be approaching situations more maturely and calmly; have greater respect and affection for his girlfriend; they would be talking more respectfully to each other; he would be walking away from potentially dangerous situations; taking more responsibility for what happens in his life; and thinking ahead more about how a situation could develop. But he struggled to locate any exceptions of when this behaviour had been applied within stressful and difficult situations.

This was his first session at which his support worker was also present, so Jackie directed exceptions questions at her and she quickly came up with a recent example of when they had been on a trip with some other young people and some of the females had been winding him up, but Paul had remained calm. Jackie acknowledged how particularly difficult this had been as he had been in a confined space (minibus). The conversation then centred on extracting specific details of how he had managed to sit calmly in this situation, thus providing him with some beginning detail of the ways which were unique to him in remaining calm in stressful situations.

Helpful questions included:

- So on this occasion of staying calm, what were you doing?
- What were you thinking?
- What were you saying?

This conversation led him to remember two other occasions when he had displayed his desired hope of staying calm in a difficult and stressful situation. Paul's answers gave him some insight into his strengths and resources and how he could use these skills when managing similar situations in the future. This is a much more powerful, respectful and resourceful way of supporting Paul in achieving his preferred future than providing ideas of what others think could work for him.

Practice activity ─────────────────────────────────

Before you try this with the children and young people with whom you work, try it on yourself. Next time you are struggling with something at home or at work ask yourself the following questions:

- When have I coped when faced with a similar situation?
- What else was better?
- What was different on these occasions?
- What did I do that was different?
- How did I do this (name three things)?
- What else was happening?
- Who notices first when things are better?
- Who else?
- What do they notice at these times?
- What else?
- How would they know you were managing the situation in this preferred way?
- How can you do more of it?
- What else? (there is always more to discover)

When having these conversations about 'what was different' you may find that it lends itself to looking at differences maybe two/three hours earlier. For example, if you have had a difficult morning at home before leaving for work, this is likely to put you in a different frame of mind than if you left home after an enjoyable calm breakfast. We have found that this is often the case when we track back to look at the differences with young children when their behaviour has been more appropriate at school than on previous occasions. There will often be some reference to being up on time, sitting down for breakfast, nice conversation, having fun, being relaxed, people talking in a nice way. When we are training practitioners in this way of working, we are often asked to do a live demonstration. We ask for a volunteer with a small problem and almost invariably the small problem turns out to be one of time poverty in the morning, leading to raised voices, arguments, and upset.

Exception finding when adults are being negative

Where a child has 'become the problem', the adults in their lives have been living with failure and criticism too and may well have become very negative. They can become so familiar with, and ground down by, the problem that they may find it difficult to recognize exceptions. Or they dismiss them as insignificant now that the problem has become so big. In these situations it helps first of all to notice what the adults are doing right, and acknowledge this. This could relate to something specific, such as the child being polite (however briefly), in which case you could say something like: 'Gosh, how nice to meet a child who knows about good manners. [addressing the adults] Manners are obviously important in your family.' Or it could something as basic as noticing that they are still looking for a solution: 'Despite all that this problem has put you through, you're still here for this child. This says a lot about your determination and caring.'

Should the adults still find it difficult to acknowledge any exceptions, you can shift the emphasis by changing how the negative information is collected. For example, it is common practice in schools to put a badly behaved pupil on report. This doesn't work well in those lessons where the relationship between the teacher and pupil has badly deteriorated as that teacher starts to spot more and more problem behaviours. However, you can get round this by supplying the child with a double-sided report card. Each side lists all lessons, but whilst one side instructs the teacher to detail everything the pupil has done right, the other side instructs them to detail everything the pupil has done wrong but *not to write anything on this side of the card unless they have written something on the other side*. We find that pupils rush into lessons with a disliked teacher and behave beautifully just to make them write something positive about them for once. The pupils may see this as controlling the teacher, but as they are finally behaving, does this matter?

For persistently negative parents, we sometimes play a game called Respect Bingo (@Mar*co Products, Inc., www.marcoproducts.com). This is designed to be used in classrooms with junior school pupils but works equally well with children of all ages and their families. We hand out the playing cards and allocate a helper for young children or poor readers. (See sample card below. They are all slightly different.) We then explain that no-one can claim a square unless they can give examples of the behaviour listed, *and* another family member confirms their account. Where an item of respectfulness is agreed, this is evidence of either an exception or an ability and so is discussed in detail to make it more visible to all. Where an item is not agreed, there is scope in the ensuing conversation for the child to reflect on whether or not this might be something they would like to change or develop. The game also enables younger children to challenge older children and all children to challenge their parents without putting themselves at risk; it is a game, after all. We find that although parents enjoy the game, they rarely win. Mums tend not to gain items in the 'Caring For Self' column and we have yet to meet a parent who can evidence that they 'Take Turns Talking' as children are only too eager to point out that they interrupt them frequently.

Externalizing problems

Workers can't always get resources for children with problems and difficulties unless they fit specific categories or have been diagnosed with an illness or disability. However useful, this can have a negative effect in that the category or diagnosis may become a label that describes the whole child; for example, he's autistic, she's anorexic. Some children are oppressed by the labels they have grown up with; for example, Jessica hoped to become a secretary but, unable to see past her mild learning difficulties, her social worker suggested she stop dreaming and get a job in a supermarket. Other children learn to collude with the label; for example, 'I'm no good at making friends because I've got Asperger's.' Of course children and young people are not simply anorexics, or drug addicts, or diabetics, or whatever the label; they are people who just happen to have a problem. To help us to remain child-centred in the face of labelling, we use a narrative therapy technique called *externalization* (White and Epston 1990). This is a technique whereby the child is separated from the problem through a problem-naming process which enables children and the adults in their lives to see that the children's problems are not internal to them, nor are their identities shaped by, or reflections of, the problems they are experiencing. This is a powerful and empowering alternative way of talking about problems, one with which children rapidly engage.

Case example

Jimmy was still pooing in his pants at eight years of age. It was worse at home than at school, and sometimes he pooed in his bed as well. Although he had asked for help with his 'poo problem', understandably he was incredibly embarrassed when it came to talking with Judith about it. Rather than ask him what his best hopes were and were there any exceptions, Judith began externalizing the problem: 'How long, Jimmy, has the poo problem been making your life a misery?' she asked. Jimmy couldn't think of a time when he hadn't been bothered by it so Judith commented that the poo problem must know Jimmy inside out and know just how to trip him up when he was trying to beat it. 'What does the poo problem say to you when you are thinking about doing a poo in the toilet?' she asked. Jimmy said that when he felt poo coming, he thought he should stop what he was doing and go to the toilet, but the poo problem told him not to bother and enjoy the film he was watching on television. 'That is really crafty' commented Judith sympathetically. Jimmy agreed that it was a *crafty poo*, and this became the name Jimmy used to describe his problem.

Having externalized his problem, Jimmy was freed from a sense of failure and despair. Once he recognized that it suited crafty poo to stay in his life and make him miserable, he was able to devise his own plans for making life uncomfortable for crafty poo. And, knowing that crafty poo was truly crafty, he was able to plan for further dirty tricks on the part of crafty poo. For example, once Jimmy had beaten crafty poo in the day time, he was ready for crafty poo attempting to trip him up at night.

(Crafty or sneaky poo is a common name chosen by children to describe soiling. For a fully worked example, see Freeman *et al.* 1997, pp.98–105.)

Opportunities are provided to the child to 'name' the behaviour in such a way that it is relevant and meaningful to them. Metaphors which fit with the child's speech patterns are then introduced into the conversation, so you may talk about fighting the problem with one child whereas with another you would be talking about taking control. Then details are collected about how the child has achieved this previously – exception finding. Such conversations provide alternative stories, ones about how the child has confronted the problem successfully in the past. Successful strategies give hope and acknowledgment that there have been periods, however small, of things going well.

Communicating about 'problems' can be difficult. One of the first hurdles is actually acknowledging and openly discussing what is wrong. Naming the problem can provide a safe vocabulary for family members to feel able to discuss their worries and begin to find ways of managing their difficulties. This is especially important where a problem is beginning to seem intractable; a situation whereby either the parents blame themselves or blame the child. Externalizing takes blame out of the picture as it changes everyone's relationship with the problem. Once named and understood, everyone can gang up on the problem rather than the child.

Mapping the problem

An externalizing conversation begins with a description of the problem (identifying an appropriate name for the problem); consideration of the effects of the problem on the child; an evaluation of these effects; and then, a justification of the evaluation. It is important that the child names the behaviour as it is the naming that makes the situation unique to them and supports a description from how they see the problem: 'If you were to give this problem we are talking about a name, what would you call it?' When considering the effects, this exploration encourages the child to see the problem as separate from them and their identity: 'At times when the [named] problem is more in control of what happens, how has it affected different areas/relationships in your life?' The next step is to provide an opportunity for the child to evaluate the effects that they have been describing. These questions provide a space for them to reflect on whether these effects are something that they are happy about, or not, and as such leads onto the justification questions which begin to get a richer description of what is important to them. So, for example, a conversation with a young person who is misusing substances could include these questions:

- Is cannabis for or against you?
- How did cannabis con you into thinking that you need it in your life?
- What influence does cannabis have on your life, on those close to you, on your relationships?
- Given a choice between life with cannabis or life free of cannabis, which do you choose?
- What prevented you from resisting cannabis? How did cannabis use these things to move into your life?
- How much of your life will cannabis be satisfied with, or does it want the lot?
- Does it suit you to be dominated by cannabis?
- Tell me about a time when you didn't fall for the lies cannabis has been telling you?
- Tell me about times when you made cannabis wait?
- What does it say about you as a person when you refuse to cooperate with cannabis's invitations?
- In the times when you have felt in control of cannabis, what are the things that helped you have that control?
- Tell me about a time when cannabis didn't stop you being in touch with your hopes and dreams?

Practice activity ————————————————————

1. Choose a child with a problem where you feel you are making little headway. Next time you talk with the child, ask them a problem-naming question and then, substituting that name for cannabis, ask the questions listed above.

2. Select a child you work with who has difficulty in managing his/her anger, and hold a curious conversation with the child using the questions below as a guide. Young children often prefer to draw a picture of how their body is affected by anger.

   - What colour is your anger? [If they say red, for example, ask if it is a dark red or a bright red. Red is the most commonly named colour for anger but by no means the only colour. We have met all colours and they do tell you a lot about how the child is feeling, i.e. raging red, despairing black, sobbing blue, drowning sludge colour.]

   - What shape is it? [If they say it's round, like a bomb, you can ask whether it is a big or small bomb and does it explode quickly or does it have a long fuse. If it's a jagged shape, you can ask how sharp the edges are and who gets hurt by them.]

   - Where in your body does [name that has emerged from the child's answers to questions one and two] first show itself? Does it live in your head, stomach, chest, etc.?

   - When it shows itself in your [stomach, chest, etc.] where does it go next? Supplementary questions here would include, 'Does it go straight to your mouth, or your feet, or hands?'

   - How long has it been hiding away in there?

   - Does it suit you to let [chosen name of problem] push you around like this?

Then ask exception finding questions.

Externalizing with children who just can't think of a name

Most children find it easy to name their problem, but some children and some with a learning difficulty can find it puzzling. Ways of helping children in these situations include drawing or modelling the problem which then makes the problem more visual and therefore easier for the child to take a stand against. Where children really struggle to think of a name, we sometimes suggest names other children have used and ask if one of the names fits for the child. When they borrow a name for their problem, we remind them that they can change it at any time. Or you can ask the child what animal the problem is most like. For example, Judith asked one small boy who was about to be excluded from school for kicking and swearing at his teacher, 'If Miss C. was an animal, what sort of animal would she be?' He quickly replied that she was a roaring tiger. 'What is the best way of handling a tiger?' asked Judith. Similarly you can use characters from the child's favourite book or television programme. One young person found it much easier to tolerate the demands of his disabled brother once he had identified him as a hippogriff and himself as Harry Potter. As any Harry Potter fan knows, hippogriffs are wonderfully talented animals but require very careful and sensitive handling. In either of these two scenarios, the next step is to ask the child what tiger taming or hippogriff handling skills they already have, and what skills they need to develop.

For children with learning difficulties, we often use an extension of the Mr Men characters. These have the advantage of being simple to draw, needing no more than a circle for the body and line drawings for arms and legs, and a defining characteristic. The defining characteristic is the problem, for example, you may help a child design a Mr Lippy, or a Miss Untidy, or a Mr Just do It. Then you can ask the child for exceptions: 'Tell me about a time when Mr Lippy tried to get you to be cheeky, but you didn't,' followed by questions about how the child did it. This can be made visual for the child by designing an opposite Mr Man figure, for example, Mr Lippy might be countered by Mr Polite. Soon you are well towards a story in which Mr Lippy gets his comeuppance (for a more fully worked example, see Milner 2008, pp.47–48).

Children whose behaviour is seriously antisocial sometimes resist their problems being externalized, as one young person said to Judith when she began talking about his problem as external to him: 'No, the

Mr picnous

(MR PICK NOSE)

Mr squer

(MR SQUARE, NOT PICK NOSE)

problem doesn't get me to do anything. I'm just bad.' In these sorts of situations, an externalizing conversation can be developed through interviewing the problem: 'So, what does "bad" get you to do that makes life better for you?', and so on, exploring all the effects 'bad' has on the child's life. Similarly some children have become so used to being described as a problem that they have become quite hopeless. For example, although tackling obesity is a government 'standard', few existing interventions appear to work (Licence 2005) although disapproval of being fat remains. Obesity is also a problem that is embarrassing and it can be easier for fat children if 'fatness' is interviewed, rather than themselves. For example, Jackie interviewed an overweight young woman who had tried lots of diets, but failed to lose any weight, as the problem not the person.

Case example

Jackie: [to Louise as Junk Food] So Junk Food, can you tell me how you are affecting Louise?

Louise: [as Junk Food] Well I've been having a pretty good time. I've succeeded in moving Louise up a dress size. It's at times like this where my presence really hits her. Sometimes I worry that she is going to make a stand, but because I have been in her life for quite a while now, her initial determination to make changes doesn't last long.

And then she's off again. I think that I have also ruined any chance of Louise going out with a guy she likes. I was a little bit worried that she was going to get a bit of a confidence boost as it looked like he was going to ask her out, but I was quickly reassured that this wasn't going to happen when his mates started calling her terrible names.

It continues to reduce my confidence… [Jackie interposes that she's interviewing Junk Food not Louise] Yeh, right. I reduce her confidence and how she feels about herself. She feels very low and sometimes puts herself down to her friends. Her friends are still around but she doesn't see them as much as she did. Now that the exams have finished, they have all started going out clubbing more, and she doesn't feel that she can wear the same outfits that she used to before I came along. I reckon that in time her friends will stop ringing altogether.

Jackie: What sort of tricks are you playing to make sure that your presence remains strong in Louise's life?

Louise: [as Junk Food] At the moment it appears pretty easy as Louise has no energy and her confidence is low. I can also be very small and look attractive and I have heard people say things such as, 'One more will not make a difference.' I think there is so much food out there that's in disguise and is made to look healthy when it is not, so I get a bit of a helping hand there.

Jackie: Is there anyone in Louise's life that may be helping you in your quest?

Louise: [as Junk Food] Her mum supports me at times. I know that she is worried about her but she hasn't really known what to do, so when she sees Louise down she buys her a bar of chocolate or something…bonus!

[After careful exploration the conversation then shifts into locating exceptions, thus asking questions to enable Louise to recollect when she has outsmarted the 'problem'.]

Jackie: Junk Food, can you think about a time recently when you have failed in your mission to take control?

Louise: [as Junk Food] Before Louise went up a dress size her confidence had increased, as she has been accepted for her first choice university and is very excited about the prospect of going to university in a few months. It was like she had a goal and for about a week my presence was shrinking as she was making plans and was much more focused. Louise has confidence in her academic abilities and sometimes this confidence touches other areas of her life. Fortunately this was around the time when her mum took her shopping for some new clothes as a 'well done' treat and this is when she discovered that she had moved up a dress size. Louise became very upset and they had an argument.

Jackie: Are there any areas of Louise's life that you are struggling to dominate?

Louise: [as Junk Food] There is one friend that Louise has who is like glue and no matter how many times Louise turns down offers of nights out they're still close. This makes Louise feel good about herself and confirms that there is more to her than her weight.

Jackie: What strengths, skills, abilities, qualities, did Louise show on this (and other) occasions that have made you doubt your ability to succeed in controlling her?

Louise: [as Junk Food] Louise's desire to both go to university and succeed in what she wants to do, law, is very strong. When she is focused and has a goal it feels like nothing can stand in her way. Her caring attitude towards others and sense of humour also make people want her around.

Jackie: What is it about Louise and what she wants for her life which questions and challenges you?

Louise: [as Junk Food] I think again it is about her determination to get what she wants and maybe achieving something that none of her family have done and having a different life to them.

Jackie: Who are the people in Louise's life that stand with her in her quest to stamp you out of her life?

Louise: [as Junk Food] I am aware that after the time when Louise and her mum went shopping that her mum has become very keen to help get rid of me. I think it sunk in how much I was affecting her daughter's life. She rang her GP and told Louise that they are going to get this sorted before she goes to university.

Exception finding in safeguarding

As we mentioned earlier, no problem happens all the time but where children's safety is in doubt, workers' responsibility to ensure that no further harm occurs tends to focus them on what has gone wrong. Thus safeguarding work can become totally dominated by the abuse that happened and the risk of it happening again. This is to ignore what Thomas (1995) refers to as the 95 per cent of behaviours that fall within broad definitions of ordinary competence and social acceptability. For example, one father who was at risk of losing his two youngest children despite having separated from their mother following the children witnessing their parents fighting when drunk, complained that the workers involved didn't seem to realize that he had brought up five children successfully by a previous partner.

Exceptions are the first signs of safety so it is important to discover these early on and expand them until there is sufficient safety that is tangible and measurable. It is important to ask questions such as: 'Tell me about a time when you felt like smacking your son, but you didn't?,' 'When your parenting is good, what are you doing?,' 'What would other people notice you doing if they were confident about your parenting?' Exceptions do not guarantee safety but they do form a constructive starting point for developing a safety plan. It is especially important to focus on exceptions at case conferences and reviews, otherwise you will find yourself discussing risk for 95 per cent of the meeting and only 5 per cent of your time will be spent on safety planning. Furthermore, the identification of what works for families to make them safer and healthier places will be more meaningful to each family and thus increase the likelihood of safer behaviour being sustained in the future.

It is not always easy to confirm that the exceptions are present. Whilst it is simple to check with other family members that physical violence has decreased, this confirmation is harder to come by when the victims are not known or when a person is claiming exceptions to sexual urges. Here a tangential approach is needed, checking for allied behaviours that are measurable, such as increased respectfulness to others, responsibility taking over a wide range of situations, truthfulness, and so on (see Evidence Sheet of Safety and Concerns, overleaf). Where there are no exceptions, there is increased danger and children will need to be removed from their families.

NAME: FREDDIE JONES

DATE: FEBRUARY 2011

CONCERNS		SAFETY
Referral Concerns: Touching the genital area of two male cousins (brothers) aged four and six. This was under clothes. It is reported to have happened on two occasions during two consecutive visits. School report of one incident of touching of a six-year-old. This was over clothes and on the genital area.	Lack of age-appropriate friendships in local neighbourhood. Since moving to a new area dad has made enquires about scouts and football teams in the area.	Freddie understands issues of legal and informed consent, power and coercion in the context of sexual situations/relationships. This has been evidenced in our conversations and scenarios that have been presented to him. Freddie named the behaviour the 'touching blob'. He understands now that his cousins felt scared and them not knowing what was happening because they are 'too little to understand.' (Outcome 2.1.09)
		Understanding of 12-year-old responsibility including how he can keep himself safe from future allegations. Freddie also identified tidying his room and doing his homework as other ways that he can show increased responsibility taking. School have also confirmed that they have observed Freddie being increasingly mature within class (e.g. helping to hand out books) and involves himself in 'silly' conversations much less. (Outcome 8.3.06)
		Through similar but different scenario, Freddie described how he wanted to be viewed by others (preferred identity), the impact of not OK touching on the victim and practical ways of increasing control.
	Freddie has begun to evidence ways of increasing safety (Outcome 1.3.02) and appreciating privacy of the victim and knows how he can contribute to this happening.	
	The family have just moved house and there is no door on the bathroom. Dad has put up a curtain to increase levels of privacy but a permanent door is needed. Family sessions about levels of supervision – family have started to suggest their own solutions for increasing supervision such as keeping doors open and Freddie not being alone with younger children, dad is supportive of this. (Outcome 8.2.05 and 2.1.06)	Dad has engaged in two sessions looking at sexual development and knowledge. Dad evidenced a good understanding and talked about what age he would be happy to see Freddie displaying some of these behaviours. We also discussed when behaviours shift from being expected sexual play to concerning and abusive and the factors that play a part in this, Again I assess that Dad has a good understanding as he was able to say why it was expected, concerning or harmful. (Outcome 8.2.05)

exclusions at school that have impacted on assessment sessions as he has been out of school when sessions have been planned.	mentor planning 1:1 self-esteem sessions for Freddie at school.
Freddie said he feels 'ashamed and upset' and sometimes spends a lot of time in his bedroom when he feels like that. He said that the 'touching blob' and his mum leaving home caused these feelings to be around.	Freddie is beginning to talk about his feelings and his behaviour (touching) with dad. (Outcome 1.2.02) Freddie has also identified his learning mentor as someone at school who could be part of his support network when these feelings are around. (Outcome 1.3.02) Learning mentor reports that there have been no further reports of touching over the last ten weeks.

CHILD/YOUNG PERSON'S GOALS	CARERS' GOALS	PROFESSIONALS' GOALS
"To be happier in my life after I have had all this work done." This might look like "being good everywhere, getting on with work, having more friends, my friends liking me more, playing out and forgetting about it'. (Freddie, 20th October 2010)	'I think for Freddie to have a better understanding of what happened and of what's right and wrong,' (Dad, 20th October 2010)	'To help Freddie to keep himself safe and for him to learn about appropriate touching.' (Referrer, duty social worker, 20th October 2010) For Freddie to increase his understanding of OK and not OK touching and to verbalize an understanding of the differences between 11-year-old and those young people whom the behaviour has been displayed against. (Junction worker 20th October 2010)

SAFETY SCALE
Scale the young person's current strengths to control the sexual behaviour

0 NOT AT ALL SAFE ← → 10 COMPLETELY SAFE

In October 2010 Freddie rated himself as 5.8 on this scale because 'I'm controlling it a lot, it still comes up in my head a few times, but I feel I have got it under some control' (20th October 2010). Now Freddie rated himself as 9/10 on this scale, as 'I'm doing well, there has been no touching and me and dad have been talking about it' (5th February 2011).

Dad has moved one point up the scale to 8. 'I am pleased that we have been able to talk about the touching' (5th February 2011).

Initially practitioner rated Freddie as 5/10 as she had heard some signs of safety in the initial home visit and witnessed a positive, supportive relationship between Freddie and his dad, but assessed that she would like to further develop Freddie's focus of 'getting it out of his head' to include moving on with new knowledge and understanding about touching, relationships and safety. Thirteen weeks have passed and more observations have been made that evidences increasing levels of safety, as such Practitioner now scales at 7. A recommendation of six further sessions to monitor new learning and continue to build upon current levels of safety (5th February 2011).

Signed	Signed	Signed

Key points

- The basic premise of solution focused practice is that there are always exceptions to problems (although this can be to varying degrees and take different forms). The challenge for the worker is to listen actively for those times when exceptions have occurred, but may have been missed or not considered significant by the child or to ask the questions and make the necessary inquiry to enable the child the opportunity to think and identify times when the problem hasn't happened or happened less. This conversation to identify specifically what was different is then strengthened by amplifying the details that focus on the where, when, what, how and who.

- Having these conversations is for the purpose of making these successes, and specifically what the child did to make them happen, more visible so that they can build upon them and apply them within their daily routines.

- Locating exceptions can be an uplifting and powerful experience for children, particularly when they believe or have been told that they are 'failures'. Considering children's successes is also the best confirmation to them that there have been times when things have gone well.

Chapter Five

Discovering Children's Strengths

A key part of effective work with children is to make their strengths and abilities more evident to them and the adults in their lives. Identification of these resources forms the basis of each child's unique solutions to their problems and develops resilience. This chapter begins with a brief discussion of the characteristics of resilient children and then describes different ways of discovering children's skills, aptitudes and abilities. It also explains how behaviours that on the surface appear to be deficits can be converted into strengths, and looks at the difficulties in identifying strengths in defiant children. As well as case examples, there are also activities to enable readers to (re)discover their own skills and resources.

Strengths and resilience

In concentrating on searching for solutions, we are sometimes accused of ignoring problems at our peril. We are told that our work is superficial, and that problems have to be explored at length or that they will be papered over, only to re-emerge later. After all, ignoring problems doesn't make them go away. However, unlike plumbing problems, children's problems don't necessarily have any link whatsoever with the solutions they devise. Even where there is a direct link between a problem and a solution, such as obesity and eating less junk food, plans for eating more healthily will vary enormously from child to child. Unlike the owners of broken toilets, children rarely want us to behave like expert plumbers as they will have their own ideas about preferred solutions to their problems, and the skills, abilities and strengths they can bring to those solutions. A central part of our work concentrates on discovering these resources. As the Children's Workforce Development Council found when they undertook a refreshing exercise on the common core skills, one core skill is knowledge of young people and their *specific strengths* so that they can be supported appropriately. To use a medical analogy, if we think of problems like tumours, there are two ways of tackling them. We can be problem-focused and get them out, expose them through surgery, dissect them in order to discover their pathology, stitch up the holes, and wait for the scars to fade. Or we can boost children's immune systems so that tumours are dissipated. Solution focused approaches take the latter view and attempt to boost children's resilience so that they can put their lives back in order.

Some children cope with setbacks very well, whether they are small ones, such as not being picked for the school football team, or big ones, such as living in a home where there is domestic violence. Their resilience helps them pick themselves up and get on with life. Other children don't cope at all well; they get stuck, see life as very unfair, and sometimes become depressed or begin self-harming. The difference between these two groups of children is not the severity of their problems; it is the ability to get a good outcome in the face of adversity. We consider it important to help children become more resilient because they need to be able to cope with what life throws at them, adapt to testing situations, take responsibility and continue to develop – whether this is a failure to pass an exam, or developing a debilitating illness, or being removed from the birth family. We avoid spending too much time on problems, because this is a negative approach that has the effect of making us think negatively about children. Thinking negatively about children does not help us discover the strengths and resources that can be developed into their personal resilience. Children thinking negatively about themselves, pessimistic children, get depressed more often, achieve less at school, and their physical health is worse (Selekman 2007).

We will explain how we go about building resilience, but first, we spend a little time looking at the characteristics of resilience:

- *Having a support network of family, friends and teachers* is an important component of resilience: 'many of life's major resiliences are acquired in the context of close relationships, particularly parent–child and peer relationships' (Howe 2008, p.107). Although resilience is mostly learned in a family environment that is low in criticism and high in praise, somewhat surprisingly, children lacking these basics develop resilience where they have support in at least one aspect of a possible network. In the Department of Health guidance on assessing children in need (DoH 2000), Gilligan (2002) comments that only one committed adult and/ or a good school experience is a source of resilience for children.

Equally, friends are very important in childhood and can provide a support network for children lacking this at home. Even where children are socially isolated, they are able to get great comfort and support from invisible friends – we explain more about this later.

- *Confidence that they can face new and challenging situations.* This confidence develops from previous successes that remind children of how they have overcome adversity in the past, which is why one question we ask a great deal is 'Can you tell me how you handled problems before?,' or 'What is the hardest thing you have ever done?' And, of course, 'How did you do it?' and 'Can you do it again?'

- *Having a sense of purpose and future.* Having ambitions, goals, a desire for achievement, and motivation helps children believe that things will be better in the future. This is why goal-setting is so important in solution focused work, and that goals do not need to be limited to an immediate problem – they can be expansive.

- *Socially competent children* who are friendly and have a sense of humour also have resilience because they are active and adaptable as well having supportive friends.

- *Problem-solving skills* are also a key characteristic as then the child can reflect on problems, using flexibility and willingness to attempt alternative solutions.

- *Autonomy.* Resilient children have a sense of their own identity and an ability to exert some control over their own environment. Interestingly, some children in dysfunctional families separate themselves psychologically from their families and this resilience is a safeguarding factor. Similarly it is well known that children suffering great trauma, such as war atrocities, or sexual abuse when very small, retain their autonomy by forgetting, even as it happens, or fleeing the body through splitting (for more details, see Bass and Davis 1988). Therefore, autonomy takes different forms.

- *Attitudes* are also important as children who can stay involved rather than withdrawing are more likely to be able to keep trying to influence events rather than give up. They also learn that stress is a challenge to be faced rather than bemoaning their fate. This involves seeing themselves accurately so that they can distinguish between problems that are their own fault, taking responsibility to try to correct the behaviour, and still feeling worthwhile when problems are not their fault (Selekman 2007).

Practice activity

How resilient are you as a worker? Look at the list of resilience skills below and then answer the questions.

1. Having a sense of humour. Reivich and Shatte (2003) say that this is an important skill but that it can't be learned. However, other resilience skills are all learnable.

2. Emotional awareness – the ability to identify what you are feeling and, when necessary, the ability to control your feelings. In solution focused terms, this would be described as not being able to help how you feel, but being responsible for how you behave when you have these feelings.

3. Impulse control – the ability to tolerate ambiguity so that you don't rush to make decisions, but that you rather look at things thoughtfully.

4. Optimism that is wedded to reality in that you don't simply look on the 'bright side' all the time. Instead, an optimistic explanatory style helps you think about adverse experiences in a constructive way; namely, it's a temporary setback.

5. Possess the ability to look at problems from many perspectives.

6. The ability to read and understand emotions is a social competence that provides social support. Resilient adults don't necessarily go it alone; they know when to ask for help and where to go for that help.

7. Self-efficacy. Confidence in your own ability to solve problems, knowing your strengths and weaknesses, and relying on the former to cope. This is a skills-based notion of coping that is different from self-esteem which is to do with judgements about self-worth.

8. Reaching out, being prepared to take appropriate risk, is also a characteristic of resilience. This means having a willingness to try things and considering failure as a part of life.

You don't need all of these skills to be resilient, so:

- Select one skill from this list that you are strong on.
- Think how you can use it more.
- What will you be doing differently when you are using this skill more?
- What will other people notice differently about you?

Conversations about strengths

Children who deal well with difficult situations analyse a problem, decide on a solution and plan how to carry out this solution, revising the plan when necessary. Thus, says Howe (2008), they use their intellectual, emotional and practical strengths. So they need to become aware of the resources they already possess that can be used in the solution, and which resources need a little more development. We therefore have an intense interest in children's competencies away from the problem, and how these can be increased. Talking about what's going well in a child's life and the strengths and resources used in that also engages the child in a collaborative relationship with you; children enjoy talking about their successes, and don't always get much opportunity to do so. Children with problems do not expect to be valued and have their skills and abilities explored, so a conversation about these provides a balance for those children who are overwhelmed by failure.

A strengths conversation consists of, first, the discovery of the child's skills, qualities and resources; second, these are acknowledged and validated via carefully constructed compliments. It is rare that the solution focused worker offers a direct compliment, such as 'well done,' 'that's fantastic', etc. These sorts of compliments tend to lead on to 'keep it up', thus missing out an important part of the conversation about how the child achieved the success and what resources were most useful. These aspects are essential if the child is to become more aware of the qualities they can bring to bear on their problems. Direct compliments also have the disadvantage of making the child dependent on your praise, whereas what you are aiming for is to encourage them to compliment themselves, as they recognize their own strengths and potential. And of course, children who are poor at receiving criticism are usually poor at accepting compliments and tend to shrug them off: 'He's just being nice to me,' rather than being able to recognize successful actions or parts of themselves. However, indirect compliments can be used until children are able to compliment themselves.

Solution focused compliments are not the same as positive reinforcement, ego strengthening, praise or positive thinking. They are simply a means of validating the resources children have discovered about themselves and put to good use. A commonly used compliment is to repeat what resources the child has identified in response to the question, 'How did you do that?' and then say, 'Did you know that about yourself?' So an indirect compliment fits into a strengths conversation something like this:

- You got up to date with all your course work. Gosh. How did you do that?
- You tell me that you just did it but there must be more to it than that. What made you stick at it? Could it have been concentration? Determination? Something else?
- Ah ha, you kept yourself away from distractions. That's new for you, isn't it?
- Did you know that when you keep yourself free from distractions that you can concentrate and get a load of work done?
- Well, you do now! That says a lot about you as a person. Can you use this keeping yourself free from distractions skill in other parts of your problem?

There are many varieties of strengths conversations, but before we describe some of them, first we invite you to have a strengths conversation with yourself by undertaking the exercises below.

Practice activity ──────────────

1. SPARKLING MOMENTS

This is an exercise developed by BRIEF (info@brief.org.uk), which in turn is based on ideas from narrative therapy (www.dulwichcentre. com.au).

- Think of a time when you were at your best, when you felt 'sparkling'. Describe it briefly.
- What was it in particular about that moment which caused it to stand out?

- What are you most pleased to remember about yourself at that moment?
- What else were you pleased to notice? What else? What else?
- If these qualities were to play an even bigger part in your life, who would be the first to notice?
- What would they see?
- What difference would that make?

2. EVER APPRECIATING CIRCLES (FROM HACKETT 2005)
PURPOSE:

- to allow you to notice the minutiae of competencies in your daily situations
- to help you learn to look at the world with an appreciative eye rather than focusing on deficits.

Look for things people do that you appreciate, particularly those hidden right in front of you. When you see them, acknowledge them verbally or non-verbally. Then pay attention to any evidence of an appreciative circle rippling back to you.

QUESTIONS:

- What do you notice at home that you appreciate?
- What do you notice about your colleagues and friends that you appreciate?
- Without people saying anything, in what ways do they make your day?
- What effect does it have on you?
- When you tell them what you appreciate about them, what difference do you notice about them physically, verbally?
- When you notice an appreciative circle rippling back to you, what difference does it make to you?

How to get a strengths conversation going

The simplest way to begin the conversation is to show curiosity about strengths by making a deliberate shift from problem talk. You could say something like: 'You've told me a lot about your problem, but if we are going to find out how to fix it, I need to know what's going well for you right now. Then we can use what's going well to fix all this stuff that's not going so well.' Or more simply you could ask the child to tell you what the good things about them are. Very often children will respond to this question with puzzlement, saying they don't know, or that there isn't anything good about them. Some follow-up questions to help them find the good things include:

- What would your friends say are the good things about you?
- What would your mum/dad/grandma say are the good things about you?
- What would your favourite teacher say?
- If your dog/cat/gerbil could talk, what would they say are the good things about you?
- What are you good at?
- What is the hardest thing you have ever done?
- What else? What else?

All these questions are followed up with an expression of curiosity about how the child achieved their successes, identifying the skills, personal qualities and resources they used, however small and seemingly insignificant. It is important to take your time over this conversation and be thorough, as children find it a little strange at first. Until they have developed the ability to compliment themselves, it is your task to ferret out their strengths. This can require persistence, as the following extract demonstrates.

Case example

Abbi is 15 years old. She has a baby girl, Kia, who lives with her paternal grandparents because Abbi was unable to look after her. Abbi doesn't feel good about herself. In particular, she can't accept praise, look people in the eye, or ask her friends for help and support. Abbi is on the receiving end of a lot of advice and criticism of her lifestyle. This is justifiable but unhelpful, so Judith has just asked her to tell her what are the good things about her so that she can make a list of her strengths to use in finding a solution to her problems.

Abbi: Don't know. Don't think there's any.

Judith: You are always beautifully turned out. Do you keep your personal standards up when you sleep out?

Abbi: Oh yes. I couldn't let myself go.

Judith: So, that's two good things about you we've discovered already. [Abbi looks puzzled] You take a pride in yourself, and have the ability to keep your standards up even when you're sleeping out. That must take some planning so I think you are probably organized too. What are the other good things about you? [a curious question about how Abbi does planning and organizing would have been useful here]

Abbi: I'm, when I'm chirpy, people say I'm fun to be around. But friends have noticed [how she is at the moment] and said, 'You look a bit sad, are you all right?' and I say, 'Yes, I'm fine.'

Judith: But you're not fine?

Abbi: No, but I don't want to bother them.

[The conversation shifts to talking about how to ask for help. Later, when Abbi is talking about her baby daughter, Judith has the opportunity to return to strengths talk.]

Judith: Even though you're not seeing Kia, she's still very much in your head. So would you say you're a loving mum? [Abbi looks doubtful] You handed her over to her grandparents so she would be safe. That was a loving thing.

Abbi: I didn't want to do it but it had to be done.

Judith: And you cut down your smoking for her. That shows consideration and determination. What would your friends say are the good things about you?

Abbi: Funny and chirpy and bubbly to be around.

Judith: And what would your teachers say?

Abbi: Some would say I'm a little swine and some would say I've done really well in this lesson.

Judith: So what good thing about you have they spotted? Concentration? Determination? Something else?

Abbi: I can be pretty determined.

Judith: Right. And what would your dad say? [in her anxiety to identify lots of strengths, Judith forgets to ask more about how Abbi does determination]

Abbi: That I'm up for a laugh. Come in on time, cook and stuff.

Judith: So that's more consideration. What would your grandma say?

Abbi: Don't know.

Judith: You'll have to ask her. Do you know what granddad would say?

Abbi: Same as my dad. I run around, have a laugh with him. Dance to my music. Make something to eat, just chill.

Judith: So you're easy to be with. What would your learning mentor say?

Abbi: Practically the same.

Judith: And your guardian?

Abbi: I don't really know because I don't see much of her.

Judith: Supposing you won a goldfish at the fair and you never got round to buying it a bigger bowl. And it got bored with swimming round and round the bowl, under the arch, through the one piece of weed. To stop being bored, it started studying you. What has the goldfish noticed about you that no-one else has noticed?

Abbi: Don't know. [thinks hard] Nowt's coming to me.

Judith: So, you can hide your feelings even from the goldfish. We'll have to think how best to use that skill if you're going to start letting them out [this refers to an earlier part of the conversation]. And what else are you good at?

Abbi: Swimming.

Judith: How did you get to be good at swimming? Did you just apply yourself?

Abbi: I was scared the first time I jumped in but it was fun so I kept on doing it.

Judith: How did you take the plunge?

Abbi: I saw my friends doing it so I walked to the deep end first to see how deep it was and then went for it.

Judith: So you are brave enough to take the plunge but sensible enough to work out the risks first? Sounds to me like you can analyse situations and keep yourself safe. Anything else you are good at?

Abbi: Tennis.

Judith: I shall add sporty and coordinated to the list. I reckon we must have at least ten good things now. [gives Abbi a sheet of paper with the numbers 11–20 written down one side] Here's some homework for you to do, find out another ten good things about yourself so that we can use them in your plan for getting back on track.

They book the next appointment with Abbi's learning mentor who asks how she got on. Abbi tells her about the good things homework and shows her the sheet. Her learning mentor immediately tells her what she considers to be good things about Abbi. Many of these are about her chirpiness but she also adds that Abbi has an endearing quality and that she's the sort of person that people don't give up on. Abbi writes all these down. As she leaves, Abbi says, 'I'm going to do this tonight. I'm interested.'

The inclusion of others in identifying, recognizing and authenticating strengths contributes greatly with regards to how children perceive themselves. A technique derived from narrative therapy employs creative audiences to do just that by asking a person who is connected to the young people to identify those times when the young person has behaved in a way that mirrors their 'preferred identity'. When adopting this idea with families and/or professionals it may be necessary to do some preparatory work as it is imperative that it doesn't become a forum for offloading what isn't going well. Below is an example of a letter that Jackie sent to an independent visitor when she was working with a young person who had been placed in residential care following a career taking cars without their owners' permission (TWOC, Taken Without Consent), racing them over speed bumps on the estate where he lived, and then burning them out.

Dear Simon

As you are aware I have been working with Tom for several months to support him in controlling The TWOCing *problem. During our work together, I have heard and been witness to some wonderful moments and interesting thoughts about Tom, in particular about the strengths and values he can present in some situations (e.g. responsibility, respect, caring, sensible). I would be interested to hear of other stories that you have of these strengths. Therefore I would appreciate it if you could consider these questions:*

- *What stories can you think of that remind you of these qualities?*
- *What other strengths, values and qualities have you noticed?*
- *How long ago did you notice?*
- *What does this say to you about Tom?*

I look forward to hearing your thoughts.

Children can be encouraged to recognize their strengths at all points of your conversation with them. This might be something as simple as responding to a child's comment about what they had been doing over the weekend. For example, a child telling you about a camping trip provides you with the opportunity to ask lots of new questions about strengths and resources: did the child help put up the tent? Have they done this before, or is it new? How did they work with other people to get the tent up? Where the child is physically disabled, questions could be less about team work and more about adaptability: have they slept in a tent before? What was it like, sleeping on a camp bed instead of their own one? How did they handle this? The more sparkling moments a child experiences – 'I did it!' moments – the more they learn to have confidence in their own abilities to meet difficult situations, and the more resilient they become. As we mentioned earlier, these sorts of conversations provide a balance for those children who are overwhelmed with failure. However, some children have been thought about negatively for long periods of time so deficiencies may need to be addressed before competencies can be highlighted.

Turning deficits into strengths

Diagnoses are only helpful to children when they point very clearly to a solution: for example, a child who fails to grow because of a hormone deficiency. Diagnoses are more frequently helpful to adults because they provide an explanation for the child's condition or behaviour and access to resources, such as a disabled living allowance. When there is no clear solution, or a number of possible ones, diagnoses can cripple children. Where a child has become burdened by a diagnosis to the point at which they stop trying and lose belief in themselves, it can be useful to turn that diagnosis on its head. For example, the Finnish psychiatric team of Furman and Ahola (1992) coined the term 'latent joy' as an alternative diagnosis for someone who is depressed by their depression. Talking in this way with children can help both the child and the adults discover hidden strengths. For example, when a child comments that they are 'stupid,' instead of reassuring them that they are not and all they need to do is work harder, you could ask: 'Are you really stupid?,' or 'How stupid are you?' The child is likely to reply that they are not stupid, or only a bit, at which point you become curious about the gap in perception between the child and adults: 'So, if you're not that stupid, how come nobody has noticed when you are being clever?' Then you can have a fascinating conversation about how the child has come to be suffering from 'hidden cleverness', and what skills the child has that enables them to keep their cleverness secret, and how these skills can be used to help in a solution.

Practice activity

The following practice activity is adapted from Sharry *et al.* (2001, pp.19–20).

Consider the following referral to the Education Welfare Service. Though on initial reading it appears negative, what strengths do you see?

Jack has attended nursery school full time for 12 months since his parents split up and Jack's mother, Laura, had to return to nursing so that she could pay the mortgage. Jack is about to be excluded permanently for the safety of the other children. His behaviour has escalated from pushing and shoving when frustrated, to taking other children's toys away from them, hitting and kicking. The mother of a four-year-old girl in the same class as Jack made a formal complaint after her child came home with a bruise on her arm where Jack had hit her with a plastic toy.

Laura has attended meetings at nursery school to discuss Jack's behaviour. Whilst admitting that he is easily bored, Laura denies having any behaviour problems with him at home. She is desperate for him to remain in nursery school so that she can keep her job.

List the strengths you can identify from the information above (should you find this difficult, turn to the end of the chapter where you will find a few hints to which you can then add your own ideas). What questions might you ask to explore these resources and begin to reveal a possible solution?

'Weirdly abled kids'

This is a term coined by David Epston (1998) following a conversation with a ten-year-old called Emily who told him about how her imaginary family helped her. He discovered that this family helped her when she was feeling lonely or in trouble at home or school; it helped with her homework when she was stuck; and gave her personal strength to overcome habits her imaginary family don't like, such as thumb sucking and crying all the time. It also helped her cope with teasing at school, and she became more adventurous and less scared. So though this family existed only in her imagination, it provided Emily with a network of family support, increasing her resilience. Imaginary friends are not always so benign; a troubled 11-year-old white boy told Judith about his black family in Harlem. He described their gang activities in great detail, especially the number and type of guns they owned, and how they supported him when he was in trouble. As he was lonely and unloved by his birth family, and not exactly liked in the children's home where he lived, this imaginary family was a vital source of social support for him. It also made it possible for him to discover his strengths and resources by asking him what qualities his (imaginary) family liked about him, and so on. Although the family or friends are imaginary, you can still have a conversation about them which is rooted in reality; for example, David asked Emily, 'Quite apart from what has been bothering you, have your imaginary friends done anything to make your life a better life than it was before you knew them?' (quoted in Freeman *et al.* 1997, pp.179–182).

The notion that many children who appear on the surface to be misfits but are actually children with special skills arose from Emily's answer to David's question about who should go first to get an imaginary friend. She replied, 'The most lonely, weirdly abled kids'; that is, children who are so 'abled' that other children and adults think their abilities are weird. They may get teased or pushed around or be misunderstood, so it is important to ask weirdly abled children what their special abilities are. For example, Boris' family found his disruptive and destructive behaviour when he was upset and angry especially annoying because he did it with creativity. Straightforward noisy trashing of his room, stamping upstairs, shouting, or throwing things were not satisfying activities to Boris. He put thought into his disruption and destruction; he hid the bread, or poured tea onto it, or took light bulbs out. Obviously Boris is weirdly abled. It took time before his family discovered this and helped him use his 'abledness' more constructively. One way in which Boris is using his abledness now is playing the tuba in a marching band. Another way is fooling the children who try to get him into trouble. And another way is teasing us; when we asked him what name we should use in this book, he insisted that we call him Boris Johnson.

Children's special abilities exist in the realms of intuition, imagination or wizardry, or specific talents, such as music, so it is important to search for these abilities by entering the child's world of imagination with them. We ask children what special abilities they have that they keep secret. For many children this is an ability to keep their feelings secret, an ability to look sad when they are not particularly sad, and vice versa. Another way to access special abilities is to ask a child what character they are most like in a favourite book, film or television series. *Harry Potter* is an excellent resource here as the books are full of characters with special abilities. Or you could ask non-conforming children what their unique qualities are that help them survive at school or home without conforming. Some questions to help you discover weird abilities include:

- Do you find adults boring in the way they can only see things through adult eyes?
- Can you see things more than one way?
- Do you suspect you know more about some things in your life than anyone else does?
- Have adults (or your friends) tried to talk you out of imagining things the way you do? Has your imagination gone underground? Are you keeping it just to yourself?

- Will you be willing to let me in on your secrets?

- Do you have any magic (imaginary) ways of doing things? If you were to tell, do you think people would make fun of your magic (imagination)?

- Do some people think you are weird when, in fact, if they really knew you inside out, they would know that you are weirdly abled (have special abilities)?

- Do you find it hard to believe that adults were once children with wonderful imaginations of their own? (Freeman *et al.* 1997, p.186)

Defiant children

Defiant children are not particularly bothered about praise. Indeed, if you tell a defiant child that something they have done pleases you, you have just given them another means by which to annoy when they do the opposite. Equally, they will tend to dismiss your indirect compliments as defiant children often have high levels of self-esteem. Instead, you can compliment by 'noticing'; for example, you can say (in almost a disinterested way) 'I noticed that you were kind to your little sister,' and then leave it at that until there is another 'noticing' opportunity. In their book, *Try and Make Me!*, Levy and O'Hanlon (2001) recommend that you deliver ten acknowledgements for every single negative comment you make to a defiant child so that they begin to notice what they are doing well.

Practice activity ———————————————————————

Think of a child you find challenging to work with now. Now think of three good things about this child. What difference will recognizing these good things make to your work with that child? Does the child know these good things about themselves? What questions can you ask the child that will reveal these things about them?

Resilience in adults

It is not necessarily children who are the major challenge to the children's workforce. Constant organizational changes and upheavals, impending staff cutbacks, more directives from government guidance, and stressful meetings all take their toll on even the most enthusiastic worker. So you, too, need an awareness of your strengths and resources so that you can stay resilient. We end this chapter with an exercise designed to help you begin that process.

Practice activity

- Make a list of the things that a professional worker in your field does that tell you that person is good at their job.
- Do you do these things: not at all; sometimes; most of the time; always?
- Think about the things that you do sometimes.
- When do you do these?
- What is happening when you do them?
- When was the last time you did them?
- How can you do more of them so that tomorrow you are doing them for most of the time?

Key points

- As is clearly evident within this and previous chapters an underlying theme which runs through solution focused practice is the identification of strengths which are unique to each individual. These strengths can then be utilized to tackle or work against the difficulties that children are experiencing.

- It is recognized that children tackle the same problem in different ways; similarly children will be affected to different degrees when experiencing similar problems and difficulties. In this situation we find that strengths talk is helpful in building up a young person's resilience.

- When identifying strengths it is important to gain a bigger picture of how a child or young person has specifically applied these strengths in their achievements instead of simply offering affirmation which could close down conversation on what could otherwise be a very empowering moment for the child.

- When engaging in strengths talk it is imperative to be open-minded and curious about those times and/or activities which on the surface could appear very straightforward and not particularly special, but with a genuine interest can actually provide a lot of insight not only in the strengths displayed but an understanding of a child's values and qualities.

Possible strengths and resources in the referral for Jack and his mother, Laura

- Jack is easily bored so maybe he's a child with a lot of energy that can be harnessed?
- His behaviour wasn't a problem when he started nursery, so what social skills did he demonstrate then?
- As Laura gets Jack to nursery and herself to work each day, she must have good organizational skills.
- She also is a caring mum; she has left work to attend meetings at nursery school and she has gone to great effort so that Jack has not had to lose his home even though his dad has left it. What do these strengths say about Laura as a person?
- Add at least five more strengths you can identify.

Chapter Six

Scaling Goals, Progress and Safety

One of the most practical and creative elements of solution focused work is the technique of asking scaled questions. Scaled questions enable children to identify where they are in relation to their problem or goal at that current time; to recognize how they have got to that particular point; to set realistic and achievable goals for the next hour, day, week, and month; and then to measure their progress in realizing these goals. This chapter explains how scaled questions can be used in therapeutic conversations to explore future hopes and assess progress made. We also look at how scaled questions can be used to assess safety in instances where there are serious concerns about children's well-being. Case examples and activities highlight how these techniques can be applied within very different and varied contexts.

Building relationships

The attraction of scaled questions is their versatility. They can be used in any situation regardless of context. They help in building therapeutic relationships because they focus on the problem in a way that separates it from the child, reducing embarrassment and shame, and allowing humour to creep into the conversation. There are no set scales that work for everyone – what matters is that the technique works for each child, enabling them to explore where they are in relation to the number, shape or character with which they have identified. Furthermore, it is essential to remember that where somebody positions themselves is unique to them, there is no set of characteristics or defined agenda that says to place yourselves at 4 you will have to have achieved xyz. For example, if you ask a poorly child to estimate the severity of their pain on a scale of 1–10 (where 1=no pain and 10=the worst pain), an answer of 9 does not necessarily mean that the child is suffering more than a child who gives an answer of 5 (with the inference that the former child needs more pain relief than the former). It may simply mean that the child with the high score has medium pain, but it has become so chronic that they are being more badly affected than before; whilst the lower scoring child may have acute pain but feel able to bear it because it is a transient pain. The ratings will mean more if you devise pain scales that are relevant to *each child's situation*. We have also found it most useful to phrase scaled questions so that problem severity is towards the bottom of the scale and problem resolution towards the top, children much preferring to go up a scale rather than down. So, for example, a solution focused pain question would be more likely to go something like this: 'If 1 is the pain is as bad as it could possibly get and 10 is you are handling the pain really well, where are you on this scale today?' Phrasing the question in this way allows you to ask follow-on questions, such as, 'What will be happening differently when you are at 6 on this scale?'

Although a typical scale is a numerical one of 1–10, with 1 being the worst things can get and 10 being the best, we find that teenagers tend to prefer wider scales of 1–100, or more. Sometimes teenagers widen the scale by going way off the margins we set; for example, minus 50 (life is dreadful) or 3 zillion (life is brilliant). You can also have scales that are made up of shapes which start small and gradually get larger or start large and get smaller so that a child can indicate the size of the problem without verbally communicating this. Or you can use scales with pictures or characters at either end. When working with young people who have requested support in managing their anger more successfully, Jackie often employs characters from their favourite soaps; for example, thinking of the programme *EastEnders*, a young person would be asked to consider who was the most calm and gentle character, to which they would frequently refer to Dot Cotton and when asked who portrayed the opposite characteristics, they would identify the character Phil Mitchell. Jackie would then enquire where they would put themselves on this scale, how they got there, where they want to get to, and how they are going to get there. We have also used larger scales, placing the numbers on the floor so that children can physically step or jump on them. This is especially useful when working with groups of children, although do take care to allow sufficient room between each number to prevent crowding when young people decide to occupy the same number. For the same reason, a scale represented by chairs is to be avoided.

Consider that you are a swimming coach working with a young person who is training for a specific distance or race. You could ask that young person, 'If I have a swimming success scale of 1–10 where

1 is you are nowhere near ready for this race and 10 is you couldn't be better prepared, where are you on this scale?' Once the young person has identified where they are on the scale you would then enquire about the journey/circumstances that have got them there. The young person may comment that they are at 6 because they have achieved the distance within the required time on two occasions, or that a specific technique/style is becoming more consistent and fluid and their level of confidence has increased. It is also helpful to ask how satisfied the young person is with their score because they may be doing as well as possible given their particular circumstances; for example, this might be their first training session after a heavy cold.

The next stage is to consider what steps the young person identifies would be helpful to them, whether this is a personal responsibility or something that someone else can help with in their moving them up the scale. Usually small steps are considered and there isn't an assumption that big changes are required, or that progress is necessarily consistent. Although some children will take large steps and make huge progress, others may need to stay at the same number for a period of time and continue to work at what has been going well. They can look at moving forward after some period of consistency has been achieved. The important issue is to be driven by what the young person identifies is best for them. Inquiring with the child and placing them in the authority of identifying how they are going to move forward can increase levels of self-belief, responsibility taking, ownership and autonomy.

So referring back to our example of identifying what else could be happening to move one point further up the scale to achieve their goal, the young swimmer may identify that they need to increase their training hours, or add something to their routine such as working out with weights or eating more healthily, or simply making more effort. Ultimately it will be ideas that the young person has identified for themselves which they believe will work for them and, therefore, it is highly likely that even though you may work with children in similar contexts the ideas/tasks that they identify will be different from each other and thus unique to them.

Practice activity

Think of a project you are involved with (such as landscaping your garden, dieting, completing a course of study) and ask yourself the following questions:

- If 1 is you haven't even started your project, and 10 is you have satisfactorily completed it, where are you on this scale?
- On a scale of 1–10, how satisfied are you with your score?
- When you are one point higher on the scale, what will you be doing differently?
- Where do you think [partner, colleagues, friends] would put you on the scale?
- What will you be doing differently that will tell that person you are higher on the scale? What else?
- What did you do to get to your score? What else?
- Does this indicate that you have the resources and skills needed to complete the project?
- What resources and skills do you have that you are not yet using in your efforts to complete the project?
- Are there any resources you need to acquire in order to complete the project?
- What is the first small step you could take to achieve your goal?

Or

With a group of colleagues, think of a hobby or sport you currently engage in and at which you would like to be better. Set out a scale of 1–10 along the floor, with 1 = you are regularly performing as badly as you can imagine and 10 = you are consistently performing at your personal peak. Place yourself on the scale and discuss with person nearest to you:

- How did you get to this point?
- What does 10 represent?
- Where would you like to be?
- What do you need to do to get you to this point?
- What help will you require?

- Who would be best placed to help you?
- What time scale will be reasonable for you to achieve your goal?

Remember that a big project will take time and that you may be happy with small regular achievements.

Scaled questions for discovering children's hopes and wishes

If, as the children's workforce sets out, we are to be ambitious for children then we need to know what their aspirations are and help them achieve these. This isn't always straightforward as sometimes children's day-to-day lives are so hard that they don't have any long-term aspirations. Other children get caught up in their parents' divorce proceedings and may hesitate to express their aspirations for fear of further upsetting a parent who is not able to hide their distress from the child. Other children's aspirations are stunted by the way in which their 'problem' has been constructed. Children often present with a problem that has been prescribed for them or one the referrer thinks sounds suitable for the agency, that is, within its recognized therapeutic scope. The following case example shows how scaled questions were used to help a young person redefine his problem as seen by others, identify his aspirations, increase his self-confidence in carrying out his own solution, and make a successful life transition.

Case example ───────────────────────────

Jackie initially began work with Stuart under the assumption (referral information) that he wanted support in 'keeping better control of his anger', but actually when Jackie asked what were his goals for their work together, his hopes centred on his wish to retain his tenancy, which he was very close to losing due to levels of noise, causing disputes with his neighbours (which was when Stuart could become verbally disrespectful). Stuart was asked to scale his confidence in achieving his goal: 'if 1 is you have no confidence in your ability to keep your tenancy and 10 is you have complete confidence in your ability to keep your tenancy, where are you on this scale right now?'

Stuart rated himself at 4 in light of the number of months he had had his tenancy and the feedback he had received from his worker with regards to how he was managing his budget and keeping on top on his bills. By Jackie asking Stuart to scale where he was in relation to his goal, and specifically his confidence in reaching this, he was provided with the opportunity to begin to understand and talk about his situation calmly as well as noticing what had been going well and his successes (in relation to his goal).

When Jackie enquired, 'What would need to be different/what needs to happen to get your confidence in your ability up to 5?', Stuart identified that to move closer to his goal of keeping his tenancy he needed to stop allowing his friend to stay over regularly. This not only contravened his tenancy agreement, but also when his friend stayed he played music too loud and it was this which was causing annoyance with the neighbours. Stuart concluded that if he increased his confidence he would feel better equipped to say no and that this in turn would contribute and increase the possibility of him retaining his tenancy.

This realization led Stuart to talk about times when his confidence was at a level that he was pleased with and when he had been able to say no. Jackie asked him what was different at these times and how he prepared himself mentally. This gave Stuart the opportunity to recognize, plan and rehearse the process for when he would need to tackle the issue. This is not something that was achieved overnight. Stuart had to build up to feeling able to say no but, because of the fraught relationship that was emerging between him and the housing department, this was something that had to be addressed quite quickly and, therefore, Stuart decided that he would simply have to avoid his friend or not answer the door. He also independently sought the help of a tenancy support worker who wrote a letter for Stuart so that if he bumped into his friend he had something to support him when explaining the reasons why he could no longer stay over.

Jackie also held conversations with Stuart around respectful friendships as he ran the risk of losing a friend and young people moving into their own accommodation for the first time easily become prey to loneliness and enter into unsuitable friendships. Discussing friendships with young people requires great tact but there are lots of questions you can ask:

- What are the most important things you get from friends?
- Could you expect all your friends to be able to do all these things?
- Who are your most supportive friends?
- Are there different sorts of friends?
- Can a person expect the same sort of commitment from all their friends?
- Are some of your friends friends to trouble rather than friends to you?
- On a friendship scale, where 1 is your friend takes but never gives and 10 is your friend helps you when you need it, where is your friendship on this scale today?
- On a friendship scale where 1 is your friend is fun to be with but totally unreliable and 10 is your friend is great fun and totally reliable, where is your friendship on this scale today?

When parents divorce, children may refuse to see the non-resident parent because they are angry with them. Or they may refuse because they know that the resident parent will be upset by contact. Sometimes the resident parent and non-resident parent may be so unable to separate difficulties around their broken marital relationship from their ongoing parental relationship that the child is actively encouraged to take sides. In such instances it is difficult to ascertain accurately what a child's *best* hopes and wishes are, although we can guess that they mostly want the conflict and upset to stop and to continue seeing both parents. In these instances scaled circular questions can be used to minimize the unspoken influence of the parent who is consciously or unconsciously sabotaging the child's relationship with the other parent. For example, you could ask the children to rate themselves on a scale 'Where 1 is you are not bothered if you never see your mum/dad again and 10 is it is the most important thing in your life,' and the parent to rate themselves on a scale 'Where 1 is you are not bothered if your children never see their father/mother again and 10 is it is the most important thing in your life.' As in the circular miracle question outlined in Chapter 3, you ask them to ensure no-one can see what they are writing. Then you ask them to guess what score other family members have decided upon. It is unlikely that a child who is being heavily influenced by a parent will score themselves at 10, but there will be sufficient difference in scores across all family members for you to begin having a conversation about what will be happening differently when they can all agree on the highest score, and what needs to happen next.

Children enjoy answering scaled questions and often invent some of their own. For example, eight-year-old Holly followed up her score on a circular 'contact with mum' question by saying that she would be at 6 on a scale of how much she enjoyed contact with mum when her dad was talking nicely on the phone when mum rang up to make arrangements for contact. She then drew him a scale with smiley and grumpy faces on it, and this turned into a chart she completed over the period of a week. Needless to say, her dad was ensuring that he got all smiley faces by the end of the week. He remarked that he hadn't been aware of how he was speaking to his ex-wife until he started monitoring himself for Holly's chart.

It is all too easy for a residential parent to protest that he/she is doing all they can to promote contact with the other parent but that the child is reluctant to go – 'I do want him to see his dad but I don't want to force him' – when the child is actually picking on up on messages that going for contact will make mum/dad miserable/cross and there will be an atmosphere and/or a grilling on their return. Some scaled questions that help in these situations include:

- If 1 is you are just going through the motions over contact, and 10 is you are doing everything in your power to make sure that your children maintain a good relationship with their mum/dad, how many points would you give yourself?
- What are the things you are doing that helped you get to this point?
- Can you do more of them?
- Where would your ex place you on the scale?
- Where do you think the children would place you on the scale?
- When contact is going well, what would I see/hear differently if I were a fly on the wall?
- What would your children say you will be doing differently when contact is going well?

Case example ——————————————————

Holly, who we have already met, and her 13-year-old brother Jonathan, had expressed their views on what their parents would be doing differently when contact was going better: being polite to each other and more flexible about contact arrangements. Mum and dad were more polite with each other, but remained inflexible about contact. Mum, especially, didn't want to lose out on what she considered to be 'her time with the children' even though this meant that Holly was missing Saturday swimming classes and Jonathan was missing Friday night hip hop dance sessions. The following is an extract from a session a week later:

Judith: If I have a scale where 1 is your dad doesn't listen to you at all, and 10 is he always listens to what you have to say [he might not agree with what you have said, but he listens], how many points does your dad get today?

Holly: I'd say 8 because he did listen when I said about how to talk to mum when she rings up. And he's promised to change his shifts so he can take me to swimming.

Jonathan: I give him 7.

Judith: Is this because you agree with Holly's reasons, or do you have reasons of your own?

Jonathan: My own. He gets 7 because he's letting me make my own decisions more and not being so over-protective.

Judith: Those are big scores. Are they big enough for you or do you want them higher? [both children look at dad and hesitate]

Dad: I'm listening. You can say if you want more listening. I surprised myself; it was much easier letting go a bit more with Jonathan than I thought it would be [Holly moves from her place on the sofa next to Jonathan and climbs on to her dad's knee].

Jonathan: We're okay with how it is with dad. But mum could listen to us a bit more.

Judith: So, using the same scale, how many points does mum get?

Holly: 4.

Jonathan: No, 3. We want to go to more interesting places [during contact]. We don't want to sit about with her mum and sisters. I know they want to see us, like, but it's just not what we want to do all the time.

Holly: And I'd like her to stop losing her temper with Jonathan.

Jonathan: She says I've got an attitude but I don't see why she needs to shout at me. If she'd just let me go out and kick a ball about with my mates, I'd be fine.

Holly: But she says she only sees us every other weekend so we have to stop in with her and it's boring.

Judith: I'm seeing mum next week. Do you want me to let her know your thoughts on this or do you want to wait till we all meet up the week after and tell her yourselves?

Jonathan: You tell her please.

At the following meeting between mum, Jonathan and Holly, mum's listening score had gone up to 7 and her temper control to 5. Jonathan's [good] attitude had gone up to 6.

Scaled questions are also useful when working with defiant children who deny they have a problem or aren't bothered by it. Questions aimed at eliciting their best hopes need to be tailored to fit with their self-image and arouse their curiosity and interest in changing their behaviour. With young children you can draw an angel and a devil at each end of a line and ask the child to indicate where they are on the line (ensuring that you mention that you don't expect the child to be a total angel because that would be too boring). It doesn't matter where they place themselves, you will have a score that you can have a useful conversation about, asking follow-up questions such as, 'Does it suit you to be at this point?,' 'If you were to get nearer to the angel end, how near would be good enough?' For older children, the question can be phrased in a way that utilizes virtual peer pressure; for example, you can ask the child who is the worst-behaved in their class (or year, or street, or school) and who is the one who never gets into any trouble at all, and then write these two names at either end of a line and ask the child to indicate where they would place themselves on this spectrum and where they would ideally like to be. They usually choose a position slightly nearer to the well-behaved child even when they admit to being almost as bad the worst-behaved child. It doesn't matter where the child positions their self as you can now begin a useful conversation about how being well-behaved will be enough to keep them out of trouble, how does the well-behaved child avoid trouble, and could the child use any of these methods to keep out of trouble, etc. Not aiming for some imaginary perfection enables the child to work out how much naughtiness they can do, what sort of naughtiness, and where to do it is acceptable. Having identified a peer who doesn't get into trouble (but is no goodie goodie), and how that person does 'keeping out of trouble', you then have a virtual role model for the child with whom you are working and simply invite them to borrow that person's life for a day and see how it feels.

Scaled questions for handling feelings

Scaled questions can support young people when they struggle or have chosen not to talk about how they feel. Such questions enable them to express a sense of where they are and provide a foundation for their answer to be more accurate than when they are asked a question such as 'How are you?,' which requires a description, although this is often limited to answers such as 'Fine' or 'OK'. Equally, children tell us that they don't like worksheets which aim at identifying their emotions. However, when you ask someone to identify how they are feeling on a scale, they have to engage in some decision-making process to enable them to decide why they are at a certain number. At this point you can be curious about their reasons for placing themselves at that number and then move on to scaled questions about how they can manage these feelings better. Our emphasis is always that a person can't help how they feel but they can help how they 'do feelings', that is, how they react behaviourally to strong feelings and how much control they have in these situations.

Children, as well as the adults in their lives, often tell us that their problem is one of low self-esteem. Although this a popular term, it isn't actually very helpful because anyone's self-esteem will vary from context to context, from day to day, and it is possible to have both high and low self-esteem at the same time. This is especially true of disruptive and disobedient schoolchildren who are often highly regarded by other pupils but have low educational aspirations and achievements (see, for example, Keira in Chapter 1). In order to obtain the detail needed for the young person to decide which part of their self-esteem needs more work, we use a 'best person' scale: 'If 100 is the best person you can be, where would you place yourself on this scale today?' This is followed up with a 1–10 'How satisfied are you with this score' scale, and then, 'What will you be doing differently when you are at a point higher?'

Badly behaved children are much complained-about which tends to push children to become either more defiant or depressed, or both, so we use scales to take the misery of constant complaint out of the situation and focus on specific complained about behaviours. These are usually to do with lack of respectfulness, responsibility taking and truthfulness and the scale is constructed so that the extremes exclude the child's current behaviour; for example, 'If 1 is you never, ever, tell the truth and 10 is you never, ever, tell a lie, where are you on this scale today?' This is a fun scale to do because children tend to be honest in their answers (we have yet to meet a child who claims to be totally truthful) but you can act rather stupid and say something like: 'Oh dear, if you do tell lies occasionally, how do I know whether this answer is true or not?' Most children laugh and relax and show a much greater capacity for telling the truth than their complaining adults realized. Then it becomes much easier for the child to answer a follow-up question such as, 'You put yourself at 6 and your support worker puts you at 4. What will you be doing differently that will show your support worker that you are at 6?'

With angry children, it is helpful to talk first of all about how anger affects them before devising a general scale. We ask children what the first sign is of anger coming on, where in their body it first shows itself. We are constantly amazed at how varied anger is from child to child. One child's anger will start with a butterfly sensation in the stomach, another child's face will go red, and another child's anger will start with buzzing thoughts. Mapping the physical and mental aspects of anger with children helps them work out whether you are both working on a sad anger, or a burning frustration, or a blazing temper – the list of possibilities is endless, as are the solutions that the child will devise (for questions about anger, see Chapter 4). Once you have an idea what form the child's anger takes, then you can devise a scale that is appropriate to the specific situation. For example, 'If 1 is the bright red bomb could go off any time and 10 is it has been completely defused, where is it on this scale today?' Or 'If 1 is the black triangle that can sneak out of the back of your head any time it likes, and 10 is when your head has got rid of it completely, what is the situation today?'

Initial scaled questions are followed up in ways that relate to the conversation you are having. For example, if the child has some control over their reactions to strong feelings, then you can move on to how they did it, can they do more of it, and who will notice that they have done more of it questions. Often, a child needs a helping team. This is not a team of professionals chosen by an adult; it a team chosen by the child. We often ask children to make a helping hand by drawing round their hand and writing the name of someone who they trust can help them on each digit. Often children name parents and teachers but it is not unusual for them to include pets, favourite toys (especially with very young children) and, occasionally, imaginary friends.

Case example

Tim has Asperger's syndrome and mild learning difficulties. He doesn't always know what behaviour is appropriate (especially as he matures sexually), and is on the verge of being excluded from school for temper tantrums.

On a temper taming scale (where 1 = the worst temper ever and 10 = completely calm), Tim rated himself at 5. He didn't know what he would be doing differently when he was at 6 on a temper taming scale so Judith invited him to consult his helping team (Sally, his foster carer, and Anna, her granddaughter).

Tim: You mean like 'ask the audience'?

Judith: Why not?

Tim: No, I'll 'phone a friend'. [he puts his hand to his ear] You have to do it too, Judith.

Judith: Okay. [putting her hand to her ear] Is that Sally? Hello. I have Tim here and he's answered all the questions so far but he's stuck on this one: what will he be doing differently when he gets to 6 on the temper taming scale? You have 30 seconds, starting from now.

[Sally begins to answer but is distracted by Tim counting down the seconds loudly. Then Judith's mobile rings, distracting everyone]

Sally: I need a bit more time to think.

Tim: [picking up Judith's mobile, now thankfully silent] We can use this.

Judith: Okay, I'll ring you. [to Tim, pretending to use the mobile] Hello, is that Tim's teacher? I have Tim here and he's answered all the questions so far but he's stuck on this one: what will he be doing differently when he gets to 6 on the temper taming scale?

Tim: [as his teacher] He's a horror to work with. Let me see, he'd be sitting quietly, not moving around, keeping calm and not walking out of class.

Judith: Thank you, that is most helpful. [putting down the mobile and addressing Tim] Well, you heard what your teacher said. Do you think you can do any of those things?

Tim: Yes.

Judith: Which one will be the easiest one to start?

Tim: Not moving around.

Judith: How will you do this?

Tim: I knew you were going to ask me that! I'll just do it.

As solutions often come from asking what the child will be doing 'instead' when the problem has gone, it is helpful to construct scales which ask children to rate themselves on the behaviours which are natural opposites to undesirable behaviours. A child who appears to be indifferent to the feelings of others can be asked scaled questions about caring and thoughtfulness, whilst one who responds to feelings of unhappiness with depressive behaviours – lack of appetite, confidence, lack of energy, etc. – can be asked to scale themselves on a happiness scale. This typically would consist of 'If 1 is life as miserable as it could possibly get and 100 is the sun is shining and you couldn't be happier, where are you on this scale?' This is followed up with scaled questions about how satisfied the child is with their rating. They may be very satisfied as they may be doing as well as could be expected in very difficult circumstances, in which case you would ask questions about how they are coping and what qualities they are using. For the more likely situation where a child is not satisfied with their rating, you would ask where on the scale they would like to be and how could they get there. It is also useful to have a conversation about how they will 'do happiness'. Children often say things like 'I'd be smiling, I'd just be happier,' whereas if you asked them how they do misery, they will have a detailed list of behaviours – cry a lot, say no when my friends ask me out, go off my food, can't sleep, etc. A close examination of 'doing happiness' with a child will reveal the behaviours which have happy meaning for that child. These usually consist of doing various activities which give them a sense of achievement and/or involve congenial friends, both of which are considered to be desirable outcomes in *Every Child Matters* (see p.9). For teenagers who catastrophize about their misery, Selekman (2002) recommends that as well as scaled questions, teenagers can be invited to consult a famous consultant. This famous consultant would be a prominent person admired by the teenager, such as a football star, a pop singer, etc. For example, 'Life is really hard for you just now, so if you were to get on to the happiness scale at all, even just a couple of points, what advice do you think Cheryl Cole would give you?'

Practice activity

Choose a child you are working with who has difficulty controlling their emotions. Devise a scale that is appropriate to their particular difficulties and ask them to rate themselves on it. Be creative. Should the child look at you in bewilderment, ask the child what would be a better a scale for them.

When devising pictorial scales for young children it is better to keep away from smiley and grumpy faces as they are either too general or too specific. Much better, for example, is a faces pain scale like the one devised by Hicks *et al.* (2001) that uses a neutral 'no pain' face at one end and 'lack of tears' on the grimacing worst pain possible face to avoid the possibility of confusing pain severity with happiness/sadness. When you are using drawings, they need to be particularly relevant to each child's unique circumstances.

Scaled questions for commitment to change

We all like to be helpful so we have a habit of giving advice, even when not asked for it. This is not a good idea until you have worked out whether or not a child needs advice – and considers you a credible enough person to listen to your advice. It may well be part of your job to educate young people on a range of health issues, such as smoking cessation, healthy eating, resistance to substance misuse, etc.; however, we find that young people are perfectly aware of the dangers associated with smoking but view them as too distant to be relevant. They know all about calories and healthy diets, but still love junk food. And they often know a lot more about drugs and their effects than we do. They are more likely to share this knowledge with you when you talk about risk-taking behaviours in a way that is meaningful to them, and not merely as a list of the negatives. Children are more likely to be motivated to do something about their problems if they feel you have their best interests at heart, accept their goals, respect their views and pay attention to their wishes. Of course, there will be times when you can't accept their goals because they are harmful to the child and/or other people. In these cases it is helpful to assess the child's motivation for change by working out whether it is a situation of 'can't do' or 'won't do'. There are three simple scales which are very helpful here:

- If 1 is you can't be bothered to do anything about your problem and 10 is you would do anything it takes, where are you on this scale right now?

- If 1 is you have no confidence in your ability to do anything about your problem and 10 is you are completely confident, where are you on this scale right now?

- If 1 is you haven't a clue what to do about your problem and 10 is you know exactly what you need to do, where are you on this scale right now?

As can be seen from these scales, the first tests the child's motivation, or determination, to change. The second tests ability and the third knowledge. Your advice could be needed if the child gave a low rating to the third question, but not necessarily as there are follow-up questions to be asked. Supposing a child rated themselves at 6 on the first scale, 4 on the second, and 2 on the third, a logical follow-up question would be directed to the third question answer: 'What will you be doing differently when you are at 2½ or 3 on this scale?'

You can also ask exception questions: 'Can you remember a time when you had a higher score? What were you doing differently then?' and 'What will people notice differently about you when you are a point higher?' Your advice comes in useful only once the child has worked out what help and resources they require from you.

Asking these scaled questions helps you assess and *develop* willingness, confidence and capacity to change without you having to get into labelling children as uncooperative, useless, manipulative, etc., and the sullen stand-offs that sometimes occur between even the most well meaning worker and seemingly recalcitrant child when both have become pessimistic about the possibility of change.

Practice activity

On a confidence scale of 1–10, where 1 is not at all and 10 is completely, how confident are you about using a solution focused approach with the children with whom you work? Make a list of the follow-up questions you need to ask yourself next.

Scaled questions for assessing safety

Scaled questions are especially useful in safeguarding situations as they enable you to give children the opportunity to express their views and participate in decisions that affect them even when the situations they are in are dangerous. Scaled questions can be devised for any safety situation, from safety in crossing the road, to safety in serious safeguarding situations. They have in common the key question of how risk can be reduced and safety developed, measured and demonstrated. So, for example, if you are concerned about a young person's binge drinking, you could ask, 'On a Saturday safe good night out scale, if 1 is you are likely to be upside down in a flower bed at two o'clock and 10 is by two o'clock you will be in a taxi going home and have managed to tell the driver your correct address, where are you on this scale today?' Or where you are concerned about a child's reluctance to give their self an insulin injection, you could ask one 'On a getting over my embarrassment about injecting when my friends might see me scale, if 1 is you would definitely miss an injection and 10 is you would just do it whoever was about, where are on this scale today?' Or where you are worried about a child who has difficulty in eating, you could ask, 'On a scale of 1–10, where 1 is there's not a snowball's chance in hell and 10 is you'd definitely eat fish, chips and pud, where are you on this scale today?' This latter question is one of many wonderful examples in Frederike Jacob's book on recovery from eating distress (2001).

Constructing scaled questions with a wide range of opposites is especially useful in serious safeguarding situations because they discourage untruthfulness on the part of parents. For example, by asking a couple to rate their parenting on a scale where 1= Shannon Matthews' mum and 10 = Davina McCall (you can vary role models depending on current news stories and local contexts), you have made it clear that you do not expect them to place themselves at either extreme. It doesn't matter where they place themselves because you can still talk about what they need to be doing differently to move up the scale. It also enables you to discuss different assessments of parenting capacity. For example, a health visitor concerned about possible neglect in a family with three small children who are not meeting their milestones could ask the parents: 'You rate your parenting at 5 and I rate it at 2. What do you think you will be doing differently when we can both agree?' This question also gives the health visitor an opportunity to talk about what the parents are doing well – after all, she has given them a 2 – how they did it, what ideas they have for getting further up the scale, what help the parents need, and (most importantly) what the health visitor considers to be good enough. In constructing the safety scale, you need to spell out exactly what 1 represents. This could be a formal child protection referral to social care or it could be the need to begin care proceedings, or – where these are already underway – it could be a recommendation for adoption. Equally, what 10 will look like needs to be made explicit. This should be something that is measurable, not the absence of something. For example, rather than say it will be when the parents have stopped drinking, you would set the measure in achievable terms, that is, mum and dad will make sure that they have a responsible babysitter when they go out to the pub. Or mum and dad will be sober when they have charge of their kids. Or mum and dad will only spend money on drink when they have some spare from the food and rent budget. To make sure that the parents don't think that they only need to do one thing to allay your concerns, it is important that all your concerns are reflected in the 10. For example, our health visitor's 10 would probably also include:

- The children are meeting their milestones (i.e. the three-year-old will be talking in simple sentences).
- The six-year-old is arriving at school on time.
- The children are wearing clean clothes that fit them.
- There is nourishing food in the fridge and/or cupboard at all times. And so on.

With this sort of scale parents know exactly what the worst is that could happen to them and what they need to do to avoid this worst case scenario. It also provides them with a means of measuring progress as the scale is revisited with them.

Case example

Linette has been persistently racially harassed by a neighbour and usually retaliates verbally, but this time she attacked him in the street and got herself arrested and held overnight. Her two children were accommodated in foster care and then made the subject of an Interim Care Order. Linette has been involved with social care for a long time, mainly for involving the children in her arguments with neighbours and professionals. The court want to know how she will manage her emotional responses when stressed so that the children are not affected by them; and how she will be able to work with the professionals who are trying to help her so that the children can be returned to her care. These are reasonable but rather vague goals; for example, exactly what will Linette be doing when she is managing her emotional responses? Scaled questions can help her to discover this for herself.

Linette referred to her inappropriate responses to stressful situations as her 'tipping point to frustration'. She rated herself at about 5 or 6 on a scale where 1 was she had no control over her tipping point and 10 was she had complete control and was certain that she wouldn't tip over. She worked out for herself what 10 would be like in terms of observable behaviours:

- She will be calm and peaceful.
- She will have good relationships with her children's school teachers.
- The children will be attending school regularly.
- She will be on cordial terms with her neighbours.
- She will work well with a community support worker.
- She will be appropriately assertive when faced with racist comments.

Linette chose to work on being calm and peaceful as her first step to regaining the care of her children.

Practice activity ——————————————————————

Devise a set of scaled questions that will help Linette have a clear idea of what being calm and peaceful will look like, and what she needs to do to get there.

Where one parent is physically and/or sexually abusive to either the children or the other parent, or both, you can ask the parents: 'On a scale of how safe are your kids from you, if 1 is not at all safe and 10 is completely safe from you, where you do place your children on this scale'? You could then ask the vulnerable family members where they place themselves on the same scale. If the abusive adult has said 10, the child only needs to say 9 to promote a discussion about what that parent will be doing differently when they both say 10. This allows vulnerable family members an opportunity to make a safe challenge to the abusive parent. Or you may wish to ask the abusive parent what evidence they have for their score, how it can be measured, and who would notice, etc.

It is not unusual in child protection work for parents to disagree completely with assessing professionals and hotly dispute 'the facts'. This does not mean that that the parents are 'in denial'; it simply means that they don't want to admit what they have done for a variety of sound reasons, including shame and the possible criminal and social consequences of disclosing fully. Or the parent may own up to one incident but persist in telling you that it will not happen again. In these instances you can still ask scaled questions: for example, 'If 1 is you are running a grave risk of being the subject of allegations again, and 10 is there is no chance at all for anyone to make an allegation against you, where are you on this scale'? And, of course, you would follow this up with a scaled question around evidence, such as, 'When you are asking the judge not to grant a care order, what will you say that will convince him/her that your child is completely safe with you?'

Practice activity ——————————————————————

Select a family with whom you are working and where you are frustrated with their lack of cooperation. With the help of at least two colleagues, construct a set of scaled questions that will allow you to begin talking about your concerns in a way that will engage their interest.

Be creative

Although children often use smiley faces when they design scales for other people, we don't use them because, like worksheets, children find them babyish and they remind them of school. And, we would guess, no child wants to get a grumpy face. Instead we ask children to choose stickers from stock we carry around with us and use these to measure progress. Below is an example of Annie's progress chart. The three behaviours she hopes to improve on have been chosen in consultation with Annie and her family. She has three sets of monkey stickers to use for progress in each area. For example, if Annie is pretty much in on time one day, she can stick a half-smiling blue monkey on the date square. Should Annie have a slip back, she can stick on a monkey face with an 'oops' expression so that she's registering a lapse but not having a 'black mark'. And, as each sticker pack contains a large monkey with a big grin, Annie can negotiate how many small grinning faces she needs to get to award herself the big one. These, and many other stickers, are available from www.trendenterprises.com. And it's not just young children who appreciate stickers; young people like them too and, when we are working with families, we sometimes get parents asking, 'Where's my sticker?' And then we realize that some adults have gone their whole life without much recognition of their achievements. Not surprisingly, they enjoy playful approaches as much as children do. The key to constructing individualized pictorial scales is consulting with the child about their preferences, metaphors and media – not all children like drawing and colouring. It is also important to consult with children on where they will display any progress charts; few children want these on general view.

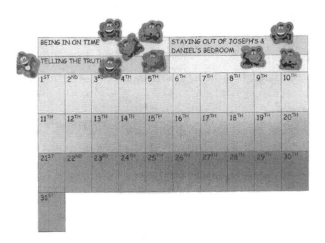

Practice activity

We were tempted to invite you to co-construct a progress chart with a child but, instead, we end this chapter with an altogether more difficult exercise.

Imagine that a family/young person(s) you are currently working with is interviewed about the usefulness of your support/ intervention. On a scale of 1–10, with 1 = it was no help at all and 10 = it was everything we could have hoped for, where do you think they would scale your support/intervention?

When you have identified where you think they would scale your intervention, consider the following:

- What did you do to get to this score? What else?
- How did you do it? What else?
- What skills, abilities and qualities did you show?
- What will be happening/different when the child/family scales your intervention one point up the scale?
- What steps will you have taken to achieve this?
- How will your skills, abilities and qualities support you in moving your work forward with the young person/ family?

Key points

- The versatility of scaled questions means that they can be applied from the beginning in both establishing goals and later in defining where someone is in relation to their goal(s), and then weaved in and out of the conversation. The technique therefore fits very well with the general fluidity of the approach.

- Scaled questions are also attractive to use as they can be applied within different contexts alongside the actual scale being designed in different ways, that is, numbers and not always 1–10, shapes, people, colours etc. The technique allows for differing opinions to be registered without causing friction, whilst subsequent questions ('Wow, you have scaled yourself at a 10, how have you got there?') provides a platform for children to reflect and justify their original scale. We often find that when they are given this opportunity they more often than not review their original position for a lower number. Similarly when there are worries about a child's behaviour it encourages and enables concerned parties, both professionals and family members, to voice where they are and equally important to provide an explanation of what they believe needs to be different to lessen those worries and move further up the scale to safety.

- We will have all been in situations when children and young people find it extremely difficult to communicate; this can often be misconstrued and result in labels such as 'difficult', 'resistant' and 'reluctant'. Scaled questions can help to clarify a child's position about how willing they are to move forward and how confident they are in doing so. This then enables you as a worker to made an informed and collaborative assessment about their motivation and capabilities.

Chapter Seven

Putting it All Together

This chapter explains how the different elements of solution focused work fit together in a single conversation with a child and how tasks are decided upon. We then turn to what happens in your second, and third and fourth and so on, conversations with that child. How you can record these conversations in a way that is meaningful for the child and appropriate for your official records is explained, and how to set follow-up tasks is outlined. We include some suggestions for what to do when a child isn't making the hoped for progress, before ending with a brief discussion of solution focused interagency work.

Putting it all together

We have presented the basic elements of solution focused work with children as a coherent sequence. After all, as Iveson's (2002) solution focused practice-in-a-nutshell suggests, all that is necessary is to discover:

- what you and the child (and family) hope to achieve?
- what will it look like when this happens?
- what the child (and family) is already doing towards this problem that works?
- how did the child do that?
- what resources already exist, and what are needed?

But of course, conversations have more flow and variety, with twists and turns and changes of direction. It would be very boring if conversations followed a logical sequence. Imagine asking someone how their holiday went and they start in the airport, continuing with an explanation of each and every stage of the holiday, told at the same length. You would learn exactly what they did but discover little about their sparkling moments. Instead, you would ask questions which will lead you both off on a more meaningful conversation. It is your showing an interest and curiosity that lends depth to a conversation. A story of a holiday will then weave backwards and forwards, and sometimes one part is of such interest that other details have to wait for another occasion. And so it is in solution focused conversations with children. A child may mention an exception during problem-free talk, but you wouldn't put this vital information to one side while you establish goals. Or a child might begin by talking about their commitment to, or disinterest in, solving the problem before you have established their strengths and resources. This doesn't matter because the most vital thing to do is to listen to what a child tells you before you even begin to frame your next question. It can be a trifle scary when you first set out to work in this way, but you shouldn't know what your next question is going to be until you have heard the answer to your previous question. Sometimes solution focused conversations begin with problem talk, go on to goal-setting, etc. but mostly they don't. We illustrate how you can keep a thread while still responding to what a child or young person is saying in the case example below.

Case example

This is a fuller transcript of a conversation with Abbi, who we met in Chapter 5.

Abbi is 15 years old. She had a baby girl, Kia, 12 months ago but was unable to look after her. Kia lives with her paternal grandparents. Abbi's hopes are to sort her life out so she can get good grades in her GCSEs, get a job, and prove that she is steady enough in her ways so that the court will allow her to see Kia. After a good start, she has been sleeping out, mixing with older men, and not going to school. Her learning mentor has referred her to social care. This is her third appointment so Judith would usually begin by asking her, 'What's better?' but Abbi volunteers this information.

Abbi: I've done one page of the baby book. And I'm only on one packet of cigarettes a day.

Judith: That's a lot less. How did you do it? Will power?

Abbi: Sort of, but I did it for Kia as well.

Judith: And you've done one page of the baby book. Tell me about that.

Abbi: I forgot to bring it. I did it at home straight away after last time.

Judith: And you've not been at home since then?

Abbi: I'm back now.

Judith: That's a relief as I gather you've been referred to social care.

Abbi: Yes. [looks worried] What does that mean?

Judith: It's child protection. They will be looking to see how safe you are.

Abbi: Oh. What will happen?

Judith: It depends on how safe you are. The most they can do is make a care order on you. [Abbi looks shocked] But you are back home now and getting over the slip back so, hopefully, it won't come to that.

Abbi: My uncle died this weekend. He went into hospital for a hip replacement and got pneumonia. I think that's why I've been sleeping out. The hospital only told us the next day.

Judith: [not being sidetracked into talking about 'why' things happen] How does sleeping out help?

Abbi: Don't know. I go off the rails. That's my way of coping. If I see people sad at home, I'll get sad and depressed and sit about and not leave the house, like last time.

Judith: Are you more cheerful when you're off the rails?

Abbi: Yes, but it would be better if I stayed at home even though sleeping out makes me chirpy.

Judith: What are the good things about sleeping out?

Abbi: Being myself and being happy.

Judith: And the bad things?

Abbi: I miss home. No money. Stuff like that. And it gets me into trouble. I was grounded but it's all right now. I know it's wrong to do the stuff I do but I still do it. It's weird, my head will be telling me to do it and I don't want to and then the other voice says 'do it' and I do. If I'm at that house, and it happens, I just stay there.

Judith: Are there any times when you haven't listened to the other voice?

Abbi: Sometimes. It's like I get wound up and it'll be telling me to do it and I don't do it.

Judith: How do you do that?

Abbi: Say just watch the telly and fall asleep. Sometimes I don't even know what's going on in my head. I can feel something at the back of my head, like I'm stressed over something but I don't know what I'm stressed about.

Judith: Hmm. Let's see how this stress is affecting you. [drawing a scale] If 100 is the best person you could be and 1 is the worst, where would you put yourself right now?

Abbi: 30.

Judith: Right. And if this is a happiness scale and 1 is black depression and 100 is the sun shining and you're feeling wonderful, where are you on this scale?

Abbi: 50.

Judith: The 49 side of 50 or the 51 side? Or dead on 50?

Abbi: Dead on 50. That's me, half and half. I can be chirpy then I can't be bothered to do anything.

Judith: So if I have another scale and 1 is you can't be bothered and 10 is you will do anything it takes to sort things out, where are you on this scale?

Abbi: 8.

Judith: And if 1 is you haven't got a clue where to start and 10 is you know exactly what you've got to do?

Abbi: 9.

Judith: And if 1 is you have no confidence at all and 10 is you have complete confidence in your ability to do what you need to do?

Abbi: 4.

Judith: If you were at 5 on the confidence scale, what would you be doing differently?

Abbi: I would be able to look people in the eye. Chirpy.

Judith: And if you were at 35 on the best person you could be scale?

Abbi: Staying in. Being good. Do my homework. Go to school. See Kia. I've not been on Facebook [to ask Kia's dad how Kia is].

Judith: How does going on Facebook help?

Abbi: I'd be happier.

Judith: More than halfway?

Abbi: It'd go up 20/30 points.

Judith: How does going to school help?

Abbi: When I'm at school, I'll mess about but when I've done every single lesson, I'll feel good.

Judith: What's good about staying in?

Abbi: I'd be glad I'm not hanging around the streets and in a nice warm home.

Judith: But your grandma tells me that you get bored, bored, bored at home.

Abbi: I do get bored but I can play a game, watch telly, hang around with granddad. I could go swimming, but I don't go much.

Judith: So, we need to find a way to get you more confidence about doing all the stuff that will help you get back on track. Tell me the good things about you?

Abbi: Don't know. Don't think there's any.

Judith: You are always beautifully turned out. Do you keep your personal standards up when you sleep out?

Abbi: Oh yes. I couldn't let myself go.

Judith: So, that's two good things about you we've discovered already [Abbi looks puzzled] You take a pride in yourself and have the ability to keep your standards up even when you're sleeping out. That must take some planning too so I think you are probably organized too. What are the other good things about you?

Abbi: I'm, when I'm chirpy, people say I'm fun to be around. But friends have noticed and said, 'You look a bit sad, are you all right?' and I say, 'Yes, I'm fine.'

Judith: But you're not fine?

Abbi: No, but I don't want to bother them.

Judith: I don't see how it would bother them when they have offered support by asking if you're all right. What sort of support would be helpful for you?

Abbi: When I'm at the house and going to sleep there and they know I've something on the next day, they should say 'no', and then I'll go home and feel better.

Judith: Could they do this for you?

Abbi: They'd probably agree with me.

Judith: So how can you ask them for help?

Abbi: If I tell them what time I'm going home and then I can't be bothered, can you remind me and walk me to the bus stop. And then I'd go home. I might say it tonight, because I'm seeing them tonight.

Judith: So, you can be chirpy if you want but you don't have to be chirpy if you don't want?

Abbi: Like last night, I started crying for no reason and then I felt stupid.

Judith: I'm sure you had a good reason. Do you often stop yourself crying?

Abbi: I've had a few deaths in the family and not cried. Everything that's been thrown at me, I hold it in.

Judith: Is that a bad thing or a good thing?

Abbi: That's a bad thing because it'll build up.

Judith: How could you handle it better?

Abbi: I feel like screaming proper loud.

Judith: Would that help or would it make things worse?

Abbi: It'd probably help.

Judith: Where could you do it?

Abbi: I could go out with a friend into a field and start screaming. It sounds weird but that's how I'd let it out.

Judith: And if it's raining hard?

Abbi: I might write it down.

Judith: And then burn it?

Abbi: Burn it with my friends. Or maybe by myself.

Judith: You are getting quite a plan going here, asking friends for help to get home instead of sleeping out and getting everything out. Tell me some more good things about you.

Abbi: I don't really know. If people compliment me, like I've got a boyfriend and if he compliments me, I put myself down. I've nowt good to say about myself.

Judith: What sort of compliments?

Abbi: You look nice. You smell nice. I say, 'No, I don't,' and he says, 'Stop putting yourself down.'

Judith: Do you know the polite answer to a compliment?

Abbi: No.

Judith: Pay me a compliment.

Abbi: Your hair's nice.

Judith: Thank you. That's made my day.

Abbi: I get it. Maybe I could just say, 'Oh, thank you'?

Judith: Yes. It's the thank you that is the important bit. Can you do this next time you get a compliment?

Abbi: I think I've got low self-esteem, me.

Judith: What does that mean?

Abbi: It's like I can't walk into a big class, I feel uncomfortable.

Judith: If you had high self-esteem, what would you be doing differently?

Abbi: Happy, looking people in the eye.

Judith: But you're looking me in the eye right now.

Abbi: But I don't feel comfortable.

Judith: So you are pretty good at faking confidence. How do you do that?

Abbi: Like I won't want to do it but I'll have to make myself. Pretend, get myself ready, go for it. I've done it before.

Judith: Was it hard or easy?

Abbi: It was hard.

Judith: But it worked?

Abbi: It worked for a bit, then I gave up.

Judith: So faking confidence works for you but it's hard. Maybe we could build in some breaks [takes a coin out of her purse and hands it to Abbi]. Which side of this coin do you like best? [heads] I'd like you to toss this coin at dinnertime and if it comes up heads, pretend for the next 24 hours that you have confidence. If it comes up tails, have an ordinary day. And notice which days work best for you.

Abbi: [nods] Have you heard of [names a counselling service for young people]? I want to go there. I went before and they helped me and I was fine and I stopped going.

Judith: What did they do that was helpful?

Abbi: They talked to me and I let everything out and I felt better. And I'll do more on the baby book when I think what to put.

Judith: How did you get it started?

Abbi: I left here [previous appointment] and did some. I put my scan picture in, the five months picture. Then under I wrote, 'Found out today that I'm having a baby girl.' And put in a picture of me and Kia in hospital just after the birth and a sock and some more pictures. It took me ages. I did two pages the first day and then ran out of ideas.

Judith: What's next to go in it?

Abbi: She had this tiny rabbit. She proper squeezed it. I'm running out of ideas.

Judith: Even though you're not seeing Kia, she's still very much in your head. So would you say you're a loving mum? [Abbi looks doubtful] You handed her over to her grandparents so she would be safe. That was a loving thing.

Abbi: I didn't want to do it but it had to be done.

Judith: And you cut down your smoking for her. That shows consideration and determination. What would your friends say are the good things about you?

Abbi: Funny and chirpy and bubbly to be around.

Judith: And what would your teachers say?

Abbi: Some would say I'm a little swine and some would say I've done really well in this lesson.

Judith*:* So what good thing about you have they spotted? Concentration? Determination? Something else?

Abbi: I can be pretty determined.

Judith: What would your dad say?

Abbi: I'm up for a laugh. Come in on time, cook and stuff.

Judith: So that's more consideration. What would your grandma say?

Abbi: Don't know.

Judith: You'll have to ask her. Do you know what granddad would say?

Abbi: Same as my dad. I run around, have a laugh with him. Dance to my music. Make something to eat, just chill.

Judith: So you're easy to be with. What would your learning mentor say?

Abbi: Practically the same.

Judith: Supposing you won a goldfish at the fair and you never got round to buying it a bigger bowl. And it got bored with swimming round and round the bowl, under the arch, through the one piece of weed. To stop it being bored, it started studying you. What has the goldfish noticed about you that no-one else has noticed?

Abbi: Don't know. [thinks hard] Nowt's coming to me.

Judith: So, you can hide your feelings even from the goldfish. We'll have to think how best to use that skill if you're going to start letting them out. And what else are you good at?

Abbi: Swimming.

Judith: How did you get to be good at swimming? Did you just apply yourself?

Abbi: I was scared the first time I jumped in, but it was fun so I kept on doing it.

Judith: How did you take the plunge?

Abbi: I saw my friends doing it so I walked to the deep end first to see how deep it was and then went for it.

Judith: So you are brave enough to take the plunge but sensible enough to work out the risks first? Sound to me like you can analyse situations and keep yourself safe. Anything else you are good at?

Abbi: Tennis.

Judith: I shall add sporty and coordinated to the list. I reckon we must have at least ten good things now. [gives Abbi a sheet of paper with the numbers 11–20 written down one side] Here's some homework for you to do; find out another ten good things about yourself so that we can use them in your plan for getting back on track. And there's your baby book.

Abbi: I don't know what to put in it next.

Judith: Just supposing Kia was a really advanced baby who could use a computer and she's talking to you on Facebook. What question do you think she would ask you?

Abbi: Where are you?

Judith: Maybe you might like to write in the book about how brave you were when you sent her to live with her grandparents? And explain a bit about your difficulties?

Abbi: I'll do that.

Judith: And what are all the other good ideas you have had?

Abbi: Go to [names counselling service]. Say thank you when my boyfriend says nice stuff.

Judith: And what else?

Abbi: I can't think of anything else.

Judith: [looking back through her notes] And there's screaming in a field or writing it down. And asking your friends for help to go home and not sleep out.

Abbi: I can do that tonight. I'm seeing them at half past six.

Judith: Okay, that's a lot to do.

Abbi: I'm going to do this tonight. I'm interested. And letting it all out. I think I might prefer to write it down. Like I'll have said it and it'll have gone away.

Judith: Okay, have we talked about everything we need to talk about?

Abbi: Yes. I'm a bit tired.

Judith: I'm not surprised. I must have been making your brain ache.

As can be seen in this case example, each conversation with a child or young person ends with a summary of what you have heard and learned about the person. At this stage, it may be clear what needs to happen next, or it may be that you need to suggest a task. These tasks are developed by or in collaboration with the young person. They are not decided upon or enforced by the worker onto the young person. This would clearly conflict with the underlying principle of solution focused practice that children and their families are the experts in their own lives. Whilst you may suggest a task, this is an invitation, not a prescription. If the child thinks of a better task, well and good. Tasks take two forms in that they are framed in either behavioural (doing something) or observational (noticing something) terms.

If your conversation with a child isn't running smoothly, it's a good idea to check with the child that you are asking useful questions, and find out what questions would be more useful if necessary. Even when the conversation has run smoothly, evaluating its effectiveness is a good habit to get into. Some questions to help you do this include:

- How is this conversation going for you?
- Should we keep talking about this or would you be more interested in …?

- Is this interesting to you? Is this what we should spend time talking about?
- I was wondering if you would be more interested in me asking some more about this or whether we should focus on …?
- Am I on the right lines with these questions?
- What would we be talking about if I was being more helpful?
- What question haven't I asked that you wish I had?
- On a scale of 1–10 where 1 is this conversation has been an utter waste of time and 10 is it couldn't have been better, where would you rate it?
- If you had scored the session one point higher, what would I have been doing differently?
- If you had scored this session one point higher, what would you have been doing differently?

The most imaginative way of working with the different elements of a solution focused approach we have discovered is a pictorial cube designed by a Norwegian health care company to help children manage their illness better (at www.hnt.no). Using a metaphor of a turtle (slow but long-lived) captaining a ship, the child is invited to consider that although they may be disabled they are still the captain of their own ship and need the crew (professionals) to do what the captain needs them to do. The cube can be used for group activity or can be rolled as dice to match the illustrations (for more information, contact lms@hnt.no).

Subsequent meetings

As we are not at all surprised when a child has not completed a task, or better still, has come up with one of their own, we don't ask about them when we next see the child – unless the child brings up the subject. Indeed, we don't presume that the child will necessarily need another meeting with us so there is no notion about seeing a child for a prescriptive set of meetings. The child is asked if they want to meet with us again, and

Illustrations by Knut Hoihjelle knut.hoihjelle@namdalsavisa.no

when – depending on how long the child thinks it will take them to complete the next step towards their solution. However, we are aware that many services/classes/activities that children may engage in, whether it is swimming lessons or a well-being programme, are structured within a specific number of meetings, it is not a problem; when a child achieves their goals before all the sessions have been completed. The remainder can be used for consolidating success, or as a 'bank' in case of future need.

The format of second and subsequent sessions follows a similar pattern to the first one, with the conversation continuing to build on what has been going well and progress in realizing their goals, identifying exceptions to the problem behaviour and people's solutions at these times. On returning for a second session the first question is to enquire 'What's better?' Enquiring about what has gone well continues to build on children's strengths, skills and knowledge in working towards their goals. This question also reinforces the assumption that children have the competences to achieve their goals. This is in direct contrast to the more usual 'How are you?' sort of beginning. Asking more general questions about how someone is, or what's been going on can provide an opening for people to talk about everything but what has been successful. This would drag both you and the child into problem talk.

This belief in people's abilities can be a very empowering and uplifting experience for a child. It is also recognized that this can be difficult, particularly when children are overwhelmed and consumed by the problem and experiencing difficulties in their life; however, we believe that focusing on the future and specifically their successes and making them more visible, however small, can have an incredible impact on both a child's belief in their abilities to get rid of the problem or to manage it in a way that does not impinge negatively on their life. This curiosity and notion that things are better also highlights that daily life is never the same. Furthermore acknowledging that change occurs outside your meeting with the child, and more so independently of that meeting, reinforces a child's level of autonomy.

De Shazer (1994) suggested that the purpose of meeting again with the child is to:

- construct the intervening interval between sessions as including improvement

- check that the child sees what they did in the meantime as useful, inviting them to see things as improved
- help the child to figure out what they have done that led to the change so that they can see how to do more of
- decide whether the improvements are sufficient
- when no improvements can be found, work out how to do something different so as to avoid repeating what does not work.

When children begin to identify their successes, exceptions and strengths, an alternative and preferred story begins to emerge. A helpful way of reinforcing and strengthening this storyline is to provide feedback. One way of doing this is by providing the young person with a narrative letter covering what has been discussed. White and Epston (1990) found that one letter was worth four sessions, so it is worth finding the time make a recording.

Case example

This letter relates was written to 17-year-old Steve who had requested some support in discussing and managing his emotions in more appropriate ways. In an earlier session he had externalized these emotions as Annoyance.

Hello Steve

Here are the notes from when we met on the 4 July. You shared with me that Annoyance has only showed itself on two occasions since we last met. You report that this is a great improvement. You also noticed that on two occasions Annoyance could have shown itself but you took back control. Respectfulness for your girlfriend's mum and walking away were helpful on these occasions. Steve, you also shared that you have been busy in the last week and also made a decision about needing and wanting to take some responsibility for what happens in your life. You have signed up to an employment agency, are sorting out your debts and generally making sure that you are filling your days as you have identified that when you are bored or feeling 'I am going nowhere' there is an increased risk of Annoyance being around. On a scale of 1–10 'How confident I am with keeping busy (1 = no confidence, 10 = more than confident) you scaled yourself at 6/7. You are a bit unsure at this time what needs to happen to shift you up to 8, but you will notice you will be happier. We agreed that whilst you are unsure what needs to happen to shift you to 8, you will look out for this and consider what will be different, but for the time being you will continue to practise at being at 6/7.

You also reflected on the progress of your life like being on a railway track. I thought this was a lovely way to picture things. You shared that to get on track and keep on it you need support and then you can push on, on your own. You also stated that more effort needs to come from you to keep on track. It was also recognized that you have a caring side that stands out and you reported that you don't like seeing other people hurt and that you would prefer to look after them. You very quickly added to this that you reckoned that people would be surprised about these comments and your demonstrating caring quality, as it conflicts with the impression that you maybe give to people because of the significant presence, at times, of Annoyance in your life. This raised a conversation about how you wish to be viewed by people and what that then said about you, your hopes and choices for the future. Our final conversation touched upon your relationship with your girlfriend. Sally thinks that Annoyance is present in your life because of some emotional insecurity. You said that you agree with this. You commented that you would like Sally to notice your strengths more whilst recognizing that this was a two-way thing, and you mentioned that you are going to give it a shot of noticing each other's strengths more.

We finished the session by you reinforcing that you are going to 'fill my days, continue to make progress in my life and have a better standard of living.'

I very much look forward to hearing how things are going. See you soon.

Jackie

Writing narrative letters is time-consuming and not necessarily the most efficient way of providing information for sharing with practitioners from other services. An alternative way is to use a recording structure adapted by Milner and O'Byrne (2002) to accommodate agency recording requirements as well as provide constructive feedback for the child. This format uses four sections: the problem description, exceptions and progress (what the child did), thoughts and solutions (how the child did it), and homework/tasks. Where necessary an afterthought can always be added. The most important part of making a recording of your conversation with a child, and for that child, is to resist editing. You demonstrate your respectfulness by using the child's actual words and metaphors, as you can see in Jackie's letter above.

Case example

Session notes

NAME: ALEXA (NINE YEARS)

DATE: 17TH MAY

PROBLEM

Alexa isn't always well-behaved, so she thought Judith had come to talk to her about being naughty! Judith had come to talk to Alexa about keeping safe because she is worried about the things that have happened to her recently – like the inappropriate touching Ben did, lads at school telling her she's sexy, getting racial abuse from local kids, and stuff like that.

PROGRESS

1. Alexa has been in so much bother lately that she has forgotten the good things about herself – but she did remember some of them.

2. She knows how to keep herself safe from Ben's touching.

3. Alexa knows how to be safe with hot water.

4. She knows how to handle knives and scissors safely – even if she sometimes forgets to do this.

5. She knows her road safety for crossing the road, but forgets it when she's on her bike.

6. Alexa can do respect a bit. She nearly got a line in the bingo game.

SOLUTIONS

1. The good things that Alexa remembers about herself are that she is pretty, she can dance (and mum thinks she might make a good singer too). She presents herself nicely (mum says she always looks good for school). She is helpful (she made Judith a nice cup of coffee). She can stand up for herself when she gets racial abuse. She likes horses and she has a good memory.

2. When Ben touched her, she told a teacher at school. She knows all about good touches and bad touches and when people can touch each other on private parts. She can say no to Ben now. She has a Helping Hand with the names of people she can tell if she's upset. On her Helping Hand are: her teacher, mum, granddad (she has his number in her mobile), Cindy's mum next door, and dad (his number is in mum's phone book).

3. When Alexa is making coffee with hot water, she lifts the kettle by the handle with both hands.

4. Alexa knows that she should pass knives and scissors by the handle.

5. For road safety, Alexa stands on the kerb and looks left and right. She looks and listens as she crosses the road.

HOMEWORK

1. For remembering more good things about herself, Alexa will put a post-it on the fridge every time she notices a good thing about herself.

2. For safety, Alexa will practise doing more safe things and then she can go in for her safety certificate (see below for details). She already has two safety stars.

3. Alexa will practise doing respect and then she might win the next bingo game. She might start with being a good

sport, or she might start with listening and turn taking in talking. Or she might start somewhere else.

Date and time of next appointment: Monday 5 June at 3.30 p.m.

Alexa's Safety Certificate

Alexa will do all these things:

- She will handle knives and scissors safely.
- She will not play with matches, lighters, cigarettes or candles.
- She will ride her bike safely.
- She will remember where she has put her mobile phone.
- She will keep safe from boys at school.
- She will tell mum where she's going.
- She will ring mum if she goes somewhere mum doesn't know.
- She will remember that her private parts are private.
- She will be dressed when she is downstairs.
- She will lock the bathroom door.

When Alexa can do all these things, she will get her safety certificate.

Practice activity

The next time you have a conversation with a young person you are working with, write down as far as possible exactly what the child says in response to your curious questions.

Then construct a concise chart using the following headings:

- What needs does this child have? [you can have more than one]
- When the problem is solved what will be happening? [be precise]
- What strengths and abilities does the child possess?
- What services are needed?

This form of recording of a meeting with a child or young person is not simply recording the problem and/or what has been going wrong, but a way of presenting an increasingly balanced and more optimistic representation of the young person's life. The importance of this is highlighted when you consider that for some young people the recordings and documentations of their life can be kept and passed on for a significant number of years, and what is documented will often influence the next worker. Getting into the habit of regularly sharing your notes with children is an aspect of openness that is often neglected. By taking great care in this area, not only will your notes be accurate, but children are more likely to agree to information sharing with other professionals where this is necessary.

Practice activity

The next time you have a conversation with a young child, record what they are telling you by drawing a picture of the problem and solution with the child. Make a photocopy for your records.

Tailoring tasks to each situation

Observational tasks

Observational tasks are a way to help children become more observant and begin to notice times when exceptions to the problem behaviour have happened; for example, Steve will be noticing what he was doing differently when he keeps Annoyance at bay. Furthermore, Steve gave himself the quest of 'noticing what will be different when he is at an 8 on the scale and noticing strengths.'

The Formula 1 task

This is a particularly good task for young people as it involves compiling a list of everything that is already going well and doesn't need to change. It provides clarity around the goals of the work. For example Karen, a young single mother of two small children, had been allocated a family support worker. The worker asked how she could be helpful to Karen and Karen, who at the time was feeling overwhelmed with motherhood and life in general, replied, 'Take over'. The worker established what didn't need 'taking over' by mentioning to Karen that she was aware that she had made and kept all her appointments with the health visitor as well as independently making a choice to attend some of the drop-in clinics, and that she had noticed that both her children were looking well. She wondered how she was managing to achieve this and also asked her to tell some things about her children that made her smile and proud to be their mum. Karen mentioned a couple of routines that she had implemented and spoke quite passionately about her children. The worker began to note things down and then fed back to Karen the things that she heard that she thought were going well, with which Karen concurred. The worker then asked if Karen would be happy to continue thinking about what is going well and doesn't need to change and then from this would have a clearer understanding of what her hopes for the support would look like.

Pretend tasks

Pretend tasks are helpful when children find it difficult to think of any exceptions. Pretending to do something is virtually the same as doing it and provides evidence to the child that they are able to do it. For example a young person who has an eating disorder may identify a day or even one mealtime within a day when they eat something. Or you may ask a child to pretend that the problem is solved and behave accordingly.

Prediction tasks

These come in useful when a child refuses to accept responsibility for exceptions to the problem. For example, a child may say that it was just an accident that they were good in Miss Smith's class last week: 'It just happened.' Prediction tasks also undermine children's stories about being out of control. For example, Becky said that she couldn't help running away; on bad days, the urge just came on her and then she would climb out of the bedroom window in her children's home. She was asked to keep a chart, predicting which would be good and which would be bad days. As soon as she reported some success in her predictions, she was then asked curious questions about what was happening on good days that prevented her from getting urges. Whether this is a prediction of something going wrong or a predication of something working it evidences to the young person that they have some level of knowledge about their situation which can increase their levels of control.

Do something different

There is a popular saying in solution focused circles that if something isn't working then do something different. It is recognized that this is often easier said than done; however, sometimes it is not necessarily about identifying what could be different but simply forgetting to do what worked before. Often doing just that will provide new opportunities.

Do more of the same

Similarly, when something is working, why change it; just do more of the same. When a child returns for a second or subsequent session and reports that things have been going well it is essential that the worker becomes curious about how the child has achieved their success. This richer detail supports the child in identifying what happened so that they have a clear and thorough understanding of what they did, so that they can continue to repeat the behaviour. It is helpful to explore what needs to be happen to ensure that the success continues by asking scaled questions, 'If 1 is your problem when we first met and 10 is your problem is completely solved, where are you on this scale today?' And so on.

Some suggestions for times when progress is slow

When things are the same

When children are making progress in solving their problems, your work is relatively straightforward and rewarding. When they come to a second session and tell you that nothing much has changed, there is a danger that you will feel responsible and start coming up with suggestions. We suggest that you resist the urge to do more and be more helpful. We find it helpful in these instances to slow down and begin again in much the same way as you did during the first session. Or you may ask for details about what happened yesterday, or the day before, and so on. There will be some small times when the problem was not so acute – nothing stays exactly the same – and these tiny exceptions can be built upon. Where the child resolutely refuses to acknowledge and improvement at all, you can enquire as to how they have managed to prevent things getting worse.

When the situation is worse

Children are likely to feel disappointed or may feel like giving up when they feed back that the situation hasn't improved or has actually deteriorated. Whilst we wouldn't advocate engaging in a conversation about what has gone wrong, it is important to listen to the young person to enable them to process their disappointment. Alongside this it is helpful to acknowledge that sustaining progress can be hard work. This is not being pessimistic but realistic, as children who have multiple, long-lasting problems will have suffered multiple disappointments. Once you have given them time to talk about how they manage to keep going despite things getting worse, how come they haven't given up before now, and can they predict when the next crisis might happen, you can then move forward and be curious about how they have coped, identifying the strengths that they have employed during this period. At this point you can also begin to ponder what small things they will first notice when things are getting back on track and how they can contribute to this.

Multi-agency and integrated working

In order to provide services which are more child-centred than previously, particularly to reduce the number of assessments some children undergo and to prevent tragic outcomes such as a child death, the children's workforce continues to move towards a model of integrated frontline working.

Integrated working involves you in understanding not only your role but others' roles. As the children's workforce is huge, this is a big task. For example, Campbell and Hunter (2009) comment that now a greater number of nursing services for children are being delivered outside of the hospital environment, there is a need to make clear the unique contributions of nursing, midwifery and health visiting. You will also need to know how to share information and work together in situations that are risky for children's well-being. This will require you to develop strong personal relationships with other practitioners, respect the contributions of others, and demonstrate commitment to working collaboratively (DCSF 2007a).

A solution focused approach to working with other professionals involves:

- keeping your, and the child's, goal in mind at all times. When other practitioners are being negative, remind them of this common purpose
- reframing situations, looking for hidden positive motivation
- always remembering to compliment other professionals and give them credit for progress
- making liberal use of tentative language
- asking other professionals what expectations they have of you, what a good outcome of your work would look like to them (Berg and Steiner 2003)
- repeating and summarizing the child's strengths and successes periodically during the meeting
- summarizing and periodically reminding the child of the professional's good intentions.

Solution focused group supervision promotes recognition of the contributions of others; creates a climate of mutual respect; and encourages learning from one another. One method of group supervision that works very well is the solution focused reflecting team, using a six-phase format devised by Norman (2000):

1. *Preparation:* Encourage all group members to think before the meeting what they would like to gain from the session.

2. *Presentation:* The first person presents a piece of work for the group's consideration.

3. *Clarification:* Following the presentation, members can ask clarification questions *only*.

4. *Affirmation:* Each member feeds back to the presenter what they have appreciated in the presentation. The presenter acknowledges this feedback with a simple 'thank you'.

5. *Reflection:* Members take turns to make one response to the presentation with contributors building on each response. This process goes on until everyone feels they have had their say. If they have no comment to make, they say 'pass'. The presenter listens quietly in this phase.

6. *Ending:* The presenter says which parts of the reflection were most relevant and helpful, and may say how they intend to use the feedback. The meeting continues with the next presenter.

Practice activity ————————————————

Imagine you are working in a multiagency children's centre with colleagues from various disciplines:

- How are you thinking/feeling about work?
- What are you doing differently from work in your current workplace? On your own? With others?
- What preparation did make for this working environment?
- What skills and resources do your colleagues demonstrate?
- Scale how well you understand what your colleagues do and how they do it.
- What else do you need to do to develop and sustain your multiagency relationships?

Exercise

And finally, a short exercise for any of you who feel stressed by the changing nature of your workplace.

'Moan, moan, moan' (from an idea by Rayya Ghul 2005)

Choose a colleague from another discipline for this exercise. Decide who will be the supervisor and who the supervisee. The supervisee then complains about any work issue in great detail for five minutes. The supervisor listens quietly, but head nods, etc. are acceptable. When the five minutes is up, the supervisor takes a short break to formulate a set of compliments for the supervisee based on what they have learned and then delivers them. The compliments must be sincere, relevant and evidenced, for example, 'I noticed how persistent you were in trying to get a meeting arranged.' Swap roles and do the exercise the other way.

Key points

- When engaging in a conversation people very rarely start at the beginning and give a chronological account of what has happened. Rather they break off in different directions to build upon or to provide a fuller account of a particular issue or story and then return to the initial conversation.

- It may feel quite anxious or unwieldy if the young person diverts from the context of the conversation that you had hoped to discuss; however, if you stick with them and ensure that your questions follow their previous answer, not only will they feel listened to but you can uncover exceptions that may otherwise get missed if you are rigid and stick with your own line of enquiry.

- When you meet for subsequent sessions, retain the future orientated and optimistic theme of the approach by enquiring about what is better. We are not expecting that this will necessarily be straight forward and the child may wish to talk about what has gone wrong. Whilst we would expect that you listen to this, you will then move on to what is better, however small. Enquiry with the child about their success, what steps they took to achieve this and what else needs to happen for them to reach their goal is the major ongoing theme of the work.

- Providing feedback whether verbally or within some form of documentation reinforces the progress that you heard or witnessed.

Resources

Internet links

General

www.sikt.nu
SFT-L@listserv.icors.org
This website provides teaching information and access to the SFT-L discussion list. The SFT-L list members provide a wide range of knowledge and advice. Should you post a query, you are likely to receive advice from experienced solution focused practitioners across the world.

www.brief.org.uk
www.btpress.co.uk
BRIEF is the largest solution focused training agency in the UK. They provide training for all disciplines at all levels (beginners to diploma) at sites in London, Manchester and Glasgow. They also host regular conferences.

www.solutionsdoc.co.uk
This is the website of Dr Alasdair Macdonald. It includes information on the European Brief Therapy Association therapy manual and research protocol, and an annotated bibliography of published outcome and evaluation studies.

www.ebta.nu
The European Brief Therapy Association (EBTA) is a worldwide group that provides an annual conference, sponsors research and publicizes matters of interest.

www.ukasfp.co.uk
www.solution-news.co.uk
The United Kingdom Association for Solution Focused Practice (UKASFP) holds an annual conference and maintains a discussion list for members. It also publishes a quarterly online newsletter.

www.btne.org
This is the site of Brief Therapy North East (Newcastle), an experienced group of practitioners with especial expertise in child protection. They arrange study days and invite international presenters every year.

www.dulwichcentre.com.au
www.narrativetherapylibrary.com
This is the main website for narrative therapy. The Dulwich Centre publish the quarterly *International Journal of Narrative Therapy and Community Work*. Archive material is available via a library and bookshop site where you can browse, download articles, book chapters and ebooks on narrative therapy.

Specific

www.brieftherapysydney.com.au/btis/michael/html
This is the website of Michael Durrant, one of the original exponents of solution focused brief therapy in education. He has also written on solution focused approaches to residential care.

www.reteaming.com
This is the website of Ben Furman and Tapani Ahola of the Helsinki Brief Therapy Institute.

Books and articles

General

Berg, I.K. and Steiner, T. (2003) *Children's Solution Work*. London: W.W. Norton.

de Jong, P. and Berg, I.K. (2008) *Interviewing for Solutions*, 3rd edn. New York and London: Thomson Brooks/Cole.

Epston, D. (1998) *Catching up with David Epston. A Collection of Narrative Practice-based Papers. 1991–1996*. Adelaide: Dulwich Centre Publications.

Freeman, J., Epston, D. and Lobovits, D. (1997) *Playful Approaches to Serious Problems. Narrative Therapy with Children and Their Families*. London: W.W. Norton.

Morgan, A. (2000) *What is Narrative Therapy? An Easy-to-Read Introduction*. Adelaide: Dulwich Centre Publications.

Myers, S. (2008) *Solution focused Approaches*. Lyme Regis: Russell House Publishing.

Selekman, M.D. (1997) *Solution Focused Therapy with Children*. New York: The Guilford Press.

White, M. and Morgan, A. (2006) *Narrative Therapy with Children and their Families*. Adelaide: Dulwich Centre Publications.

Disability, physical and mental health

Bliss, V. and Edmonds, G. (2008) *A Self-determined Future with Asperger's Syndrome*. London: Jessica Kingsley Publishers.

Duncan, L., Ghul, R. and Mousley, S. (2007) *Creating Positive Futures: Solution Focused Recovery from Mental Distress*. London: BT Press.

Hawkes, D., Marsh, T. and Wilgosh, R. (1998) *Solution Focused Therapy. A Handbook for Health Care Professionals*. Oxford: Butterworth Heinemann.

Jones, V. and Northway, R. (2006) 'Children with Learning Disabilities.' In A. Glasper and J. Richardson (eds) *A Textbook of Children's and Young People's Nursing*. London: Churchill Livingstone, Elsevier.

McAllister, M. (2007) *Solution Focused Nursing*. Basingstoke: Palgrave.

Group work

Couzens, A. (1999) 'Sharing the Load: Group Conversations with Indigenous Men.' In *Extending Narrative Therapy. A Collection of Practice-based Papers.* Adelaide: Dulwich Centre Publications.

Milner, J. (2004) 'Group work with young women.' *Context 74*, 14–17.

Sharry, J. (2001) *Solution Focused Groupwork.* London: Sage.

Self-harm

Hendon, J. (2005) *Preventing Suicide. The Solution Focused Approach.* Chichester: Wiley.

Jacob, F. (2001) *Solution Focused Recovery from Eating Distress.* London: BT Press.

Selekman, M.D. (2002) *Living on the Razor's Edge.* London: W.W. Norton.

Selekman, M.D. (2006) *Working with Self Harming Adolescents.* New York: W.W. Norton.

Defiant children

Levy, R. and O'Hanlon, B. (2001) *Try and Make Me! Simple Strategies that Turn off the Tantrums and Create Cooperation.* Breinigsville, PA: Rodale (distributed by St. Martin's Press).

Foster care

Kelly, G. and Gilligan, R. (2002) *Issues in Foster Care.* London: Jessica Kingsley Publishers.

Milner, J. (2008) 'Solution focused approaches to caring for children whose behaviour is sexually harmful.' *Adoption and Fostering 32*, 42–50.

Depression

Selekman, M.D. (2007) *The Optimistic Child. A Proven Program to Safeguard Children Against Depression and Build Lifelong Resilience.* New York: Houghton Mifflin.

Schools

Ajmal, Y and Rees, I. (2004) *Solutions in Schools.* London: BT Press.

Kelly, M.S., Kim, J.S. and Franklin, C. (2008) *Solution Focused Brief Therapy in Schools. A 360-degree View of Research and Practice.* New York: Oxford University Press.

Metcalfe, L. (2002) *Teaching Towards Solutions: A Solution Focused Guide to Improving Student Behaviour, Grades, Parental Support and Staff Morale.* Carmarthen: Crown House Publishing.

Rhodes, J. and Ajmal, Y. (1995) *Solution Focused Thinking in Schools.* London: BT Press.

Young, S. (2002) *Solution Focused Schools: Anti-bullying and Beyond.* London: BT Press.

Materials

www.incentiveplus.co.uk

www.speechmark.co.uk

www.innovativeresources.com

www.mrmen.com

sales@marcoproducts.com

www.interactivesolutions.co.uk

www.workingwithmen.org

www.nya.org.uk

These companies publish resources to promote social, emotional and behavioural skills in children. They are basically educational materials, each game dealing with an aspect of school life that could be problematic for either individual children or classrooms; for example, bullying, anger management, social skills, etc. Unless they have an obvious solution focus, such as Strengths Cards, we adapt the materials so that they serve our solution focused practice. They don't replace our way of working with children. The main reasons for using games is to introduce playfulness into what is actually very serious business, and to reduce feelings of embarrassment and shame.

References

Barnardo's (undated) *Meeting with Respect. A pack of creative ideas and guidance for involving children and young people in meetings with parents, carers and professionals.* Barkingside: Barnardo's.

Bass, E. and Davis, L. (1988) *The Courage to Heal. A Guide for Women Survivors of Child Sexual Abuse.* New York: HarperCollins.

Bates, F. (2005) 'Disabled Children.' In R. Chambers and K. Licence (eds) *Looking After Children in Primary Care. A Companion to the Children's National Service Framework.* Abingdon: Radcliffe Publishing.

Berg, I.K. and Steiner, T. (2003) *Children's Solution Work.* London: W.W. Norton.

Brewster, S.J. (2004) 'Putting words in their mouth? Interviewing people with learning disabilities and little/no speech.' *British Journal of Learning Disability 32,* 166–169.

Cable, A. (2009) 'I was torn between two mums.' *Daily Mail,* 6 August, p.50.

Campbell, S. and Hunter, J. (2009) 'Nursing and *Every Child Matters.*' In R. Barker (ed.) *Making Sense of Every Child Matters, Multi-professional Guidance.* Bristol: The Policy Press.

Couzens, A. (1999) 'Sharing the Load: Group Conversations with Indigenous Men.' In *Extending Narrative Therapy. A Collection of Practice-based Papers.* Adelaide: Dulwich Centre Publications.

DCSF (2007a) *The Children's Plan: Building Brighter Futures.* London: The Stationary Office.

DCSF (2007b) *Effective Integrated Working: Findings of Concept of Operations Study.* London: The Stationery Office.

DCSF (2008) *Safer Children in a Digital World. The Report of the Byron Review.* London: DCSF and DCMS

DCSF (2008a) *2020 Children and Young People's Workforce Strategy: The Young Voice Report.* London: The Stationary Office

de Jong, P. and Berg, I.K. (2008) *Interviewing for Solutions,* 3rd edn. New York and London: Thomson Brooks/Cole.

de Shazer, S. (1994) *Words Were Originally Magic.* New York and London: W.W. Norton.

de Shazer, S. (1985) *Keys to Solution in Brief Therapy.* New York: W.W. Norton.

de Shazer, S. (1988) *Clues: Investigating Solutions in Brief Therapy.* New York: W.W. Norton.

de Shazer, S. (1991) *Putting Difference to Work.* New York: W.W. Norton.

DoH (2000) *Framework for the Assessment of Children in Need and their Families. Consultative Draft.* London: The Stationary Office.

DoH (2008) *Children and Young People in Mind: The Final Report of the National CAMHS Review.* London: The Stationary Office

DoH (2009) *Equal Access? A Practical Guide for the NHS: Creating a Single Equality Scheme that includes Improving Access for People with Learning Disabilities.* London: The Stationary Office.

DoH and DfES (2004) *National Service Framework for Children, Young People and Maternity Services: Disabled Children and Young People and Those with Complex Health Needs.* London: The Stationary Office.

Edwards, L.M. and Pedrotti, J.T. (2004) 'Utilizing the strengths of our cultures. Therapy with biracial women and children.' *Women and Therapy 27* (1&2), 33–43.

Elliot, E. and Watson, A. (2000) 'Children's Voices in Health Care Planning.' In A. Glasper and L. Ireland (eds) *Evidence-based Child Health Care: Challenges for Practice.* Basingstoke: Macmillan

Epston, D (1998) *Catching Up with David Epston. A Collection of Narrative Practice-based Papers. 1991–1996.* Adelaide: Dulwich Centre Publications.

Freeman, J., Epston, D. and Lobovits, D. (1997) *Playful Approaches to Serious Problems. Narrative Therapy with Children and Their Families.* London: W.W. Norton.

Furman, B. and Ahola, T. (1992) *Solution Talk. Hosting Therapeutic Conversations.* London: W.W. Norton.

Gardiner, G. (1977) 'The rights of dying children. Some personal reflections.' *Psychotherapy Bulletin 10,* 20–23.

Ghul, R. (2005) 'Moan, Moan, Moan.' In T.S. Nelson (ed.) *Education and Training in Solution Focused Brief Therapy.* New York: The Haworth Press.

Gill, O. and Jack, G. (2007) *The Child and Family in Context. Developing Ecological Practice in Disadvantaged Communities.* Lyme Regis: Russell House Press/Barnardo's.

Gilligan, R. (2002) 'Promoting Positive Outcomes in Children in Need. The Assessment of Protective Factors.' In J. Horwath (ed.) *The Child's World: The Comprehensive Guide to Assessing Children in Need.* London: Jessica Kingsley Publishers.

Hackett, P. (2005) 'Ever Appreciating Circles.' In T.S. Nelson (ed.) *Education and Training in Solution Focused Brief Therapy.* New York: The Haworth Press.

Harper, G. and Hopkinson, P (2002) 'Protective behaviours: a useful approach in working with people with learning disabilities.' *British Journal of Learning Disability 30,* 149–52.

Hawkes, D., Marsh, T. and Wilgosh, R. (1998) *Solution Focused Therapy. A Handbook for Health Care Professionals.* Oxford: Butterworth Heinemann.

Hendon, J. (2005) *Preventing Suicide. The Solution Focused Approach.* Chichester: Wiley.

Hicks, C.L., von Baeyer, C.L., Spafford, P.A., von Korlaar, I. and Goodenough, B. (2001) 'The faces pain scale revisited: towards a common metric in pediatric pain measurement.' *Pain 93,* 2, 173–183.

HM Treasury and DCSF (2007) *Aiming High for Young People. A Ten-year Strategy for Positive Activities.* London: The Stationary Office

Howe, D. (2008) *The Emotionally Intelligent Social Worker.* Basingstoke: Palgrave.

Howe, D. (2009) *A Brief Introduction to Social Work Theory.* Basingstoke: Palgrave.

Iveson, C. (1990) *Whose Life? Community Care of Older People and Their Families.* London: BT Press.

Iveson, C. (2002) *Whose Life? Community Care of Older People and Their Families,* 2nd edn. London: BT Press.

Jacob, F. (2001) *Solution Focused Recovery from Eating Distress.* London: BT Press.

Jones, V. and Northway, R. (2006) 'Children with Learning Disabilities.' In A. Glasper and J. Richardson (eds) *A Textbook of Children's and Young People's Nursing.* London: Churchill Livingstone, Elsevier.

Kelsey, J. and McEwing, G. (2008) *Clinical Skills in Child Health Practice.* London: Churchill Livingstone, Elsevier.

Levy, R. and O'Hanlon, B. (2001) *Try and Make Me! Simple Strategies that Turn Off the Tantrums and Create Cooperation.* Breinigsville, PA: Rodale (distributed by St Martin's Press).

Licence, K. (2005) 'Promoting a Healthy Diet and Physical Activity for Children and Young People – the Evidence.' In R. Chambers and K. Licence (eds) *Looking After Children in Primary Care. A Companion to the Children's National Service Framework.* Abingdon: Radcliffe Publishing.

Macdonald, A. (2007) *Solution Focused Therapy. Theory, Research and Practice.* London: Sage.

McKibben, J. (2009) 'How to encourage child-led play?' *Early Years,* Summer, www.DCSF.gov.uk/everychildmatters, pp.8–9.

McNeish, D., Newman, T. and Roberts, H. (2002) *What Works for Children?* Buckingham: Open University Press.

Matthews, J. (2006) 'Communicating with Children.' In A. Glasper and J. Richardson (eds) *A Textbook of Children's and Young People's Nursing.* London: Churchill Livingstone, Elsevier.

Mencap (2007) *Death by Indifference.* London: Mencap.

Michael, J. (2008) *Healthcare for All: Report of the Independent Inquiry into Access to Healthcare for People with Learning Difficulties.* London: Aldridge Press.

Miller, G. (1997) 'Systems and solutions: the discourses of brief therapy.' *Contemporary Family Therapy 19,* 5–22.

Milner, J. (2001) *Women and Social Work. Narrative Approaches.* Basingstoke: Macmillan.

Milner, J. (2004) 'Group work with young women.' *Context 74,* 14–17.

Milner, J. (2008) 'Solution focused approaches to caring for children whose behaviour is sexually harmful.' *Adoption and Fostering 32,* 42–50.

Milner, J. and O'Byrne, P. (2002) *Brief Counselling. Narratives and Solutions.* Basingstoke: Palgrave.

Mullender, A. (1999a) 'Drawing out Messages for Policy and Practice.' In A. Mullender (ed.) *We Are Family. Sibling Relationships in Placement and Beyond.* London: BAAF.

Mullender, A. (1999b) 'Sketching in the Background.' In A. Mullender (ed.) *We Are Family. Sibling Relationships in Placement and Beyond.* London: BAAF.

Myers, S. (2008) *Solution Focused Approaches.* Lyme Regis: Russell House Publishing.

Myers, S. and Milner, J. (2007) *Sexual Issues in Social Work.* Bristol: The Policy Press.

Norman, H. (2000) 'Reflecting Teams.' Unpublished paper presented at the Midland Association for Solution Focused Therapy, February. More details In O'Connell, B. (2001) *Solution Focused Stress Counselling.* London: Continuum.

Orr, R. (2003) *My Right to Play. A Child with Complex Needs.* Maidenhead: Open University Press.

Parton, N. and O'Byrne, P. (2000) *Constructive Social Work*. Basingstoke: Palgrave.

Polaschek, L. and Polaschek, N. (2007) 'Solution focused conversations: a new therapeutic strategy in well nursing telephone consultations.' *Journal of Advanced Nursing 59*, 2, 111–119.

Reivich, K. and Shatte, A. (2003) *The Resilience Factor: 7 Keys to Finding your Inner Strength and Overcoming Life's Hurdles*. London: Broadway Book.

Ross, M. (1996) 'Learning to Listen to Children.' In R. Davie, G. Upton and V. Varma (eds) *The Voice of the Child. A Handbook for Professionals*. London: Falmer Press.

Roulstone, S. (2001) *Prioritising Child Health. Practice and Principles*. London: Routledge.

Saleeby, D. (1992) *The Strengths Perspective in Social Work Practice*. White Plains, NY: Longman.

Saleeby, D. (ed.) (2007) *The Strengths Perspective in Social Work Practice*, 4th edn. Boston, MD: Allyn & Bacon.

Selekman, M.D. (2002) *Living on the Razor's Edge*. London: W.W. Norton.

Selekman, M.D. (2007) *The Optimistic Child. A Proven Program to Safeguard Children Against Depression and Build Lifelong Resilience*. New York: Houghton Mifflin.

Sharry, J. (2001) *Solution Focused Groupwork*. London: Sage.

Sharry, J., Madden, B. and Darmody, M. (2001) *Becoming a Solution Detective. A Strengths-based Guide to Brief Therapy*. London: BT Press.

Tates, K., Meeuwesen, L. and Bensing, J. (2002) '"I've come for the his throat": roles and identities in doctor–parent–child communication.' *Child: Care, Health and Development 28*, 1, 109–116.

Taylor, C. (2004) 'Underpinning knowledge of child care practice: reconsidering child development theory.' *Child and Family Social Work 9*, 225–235.

Thomas, G. (1995) *Travels in the Trench Between Child Welfare Theory and Practice*. New York: The Haworth Press.

Thompson, N. (2003) *Communication and Language. A Handbook of Theory and Practice*. Basingstoke: Palgrave Macmillan.

Turnell, A. and Edwards, S. (1999) *Signs of Safety: A Solution Oriented Approach to Child Protection Casework*. New York: W.W. Norton.

White, N. and Bateman, J. (2008) 'The use of narrative therapy to allow the emergence of engagement.' *The International Journal of Narrative Therapy and Community Work 2*, 17–28, Dulwich Centre Publications Pty Ltd.

White, D. and Epston, D. (1990) *Narrative Means to Therapeutic Ends*. London: W.W. Norton.

Whiting, L. (2006) 'Children and their Families.' In I. Peate and L. Whiting (eds) *Caring for Children and Families*. Chichester: Wiley.

Wittgenstein, L. (1963) *Philosophical Investigations*. Oxford: Blackwell.

Wittgenstein, L. (1980) *Remarks on the Philosophy of Psychology*. Oxford: Basil Blackwell.

Subject Index

Author Index